CHESTER & NORTH WALES BORDER RAILWAYS

A VIEW FROM THE PAST

REX CHRISTIANSEN

Ian Allan
PUBLISHING

Front Cover: In July 1959, Stanier Class 8F No 48259 crosses the River Dee at Chester with a down freight for North Wales. The city and the racecourse make a fine backdrop to the Chester-Holyhead main line. The GWR's Shrewsbury-Chester services used the two tracks on the right.
G. H. Hunt/Colour-Rail BRM1767

Rear Cover upper: 'Castle' class No 5061 *Earl of Birkenhead* awaits departure from Shrewsbury with a weekday-only Margate-Birkenhead in 1959.
Ian Allan Library/S. D. Wainwright

Rear Cover lower: A study of the Welsh railway scene at Llangollen *Leicester Museums* which was a popular destination for day excursionists from Merseyside.

Title page: Much Wenlock was the most photographed – and artist-painted – station on the single-line branch from Wellington to Craven Arms because of its delightful setting. Pannier tank No 9741 waits with a train from Wellington in December 1955. This was four years after through passenger services to Craven Arms had been withdrawn.
Author's collection/N. Fields

Below:
'Royal Scot' No 46163 *Civil Service Rifleman* leaves Chester for Warrington and Manchester Exchange with an express from Holyhead on 24 April 1962. The Crewe line is on the left.
Ian Allan Library/J. R. Carter

First published 2001

ISBN 0 7110 2816 8

© Ian Allan Publishing Ltd 2001

Published by Ian Allan Publishing

an imprint of Ian Allan Publishing Ltd, Hersham, Surrey KT12 4RG.
Printed by Ian Allan Printing Ltd, Hersham, Surrey KT12 4RG.

Code: 0111 /B2

Contents

Introduction 5

Acknowledgements 6

1. Chester 7

2. Wrexham-Ruabon-Shrewsbury 25

3. Oswestry 43

4. Shrewsbury 51

5. Shrewsbury & Hereford: Branches 67

6. Locomotives and Sheds 83

Chronology 93

Bibliography 96

Right:
On 27 September 1958, a passing up freight is headed by BR Standard Class 4 4-6-0 No 75051.
Ian Allan Library/T. Lewis

BIRKENHEAD (Woodside)
West Kirby
Kirby Park
Caldy
Thurstaston
Heswall
Parkgate (Cheshire)
Neston
Flint
Capenhurst
Mollington

LIVERPOOL (Town)
Rock Ferry
Bebington & New Ferry
Port Sunlight
Spital
Bromborough
Hooton
Little Sutton
Ellesmere Port
Ince & Elton
Ledsham
Hadlow Rd
Dunham Hill
Mickle Trafford

Newton-le-Willows
Earlestown Junc.

MANCHESTER
(Central) (London Rd.)
Glazebrook
Astley
Barton Mo
Patricroft
Eccles
Ordsall La
Cross La (Exch)
Weaste
Sedley

STOCKPORT
SHEFFIELD
To Y

Warrington
Daresbury
Norton (Cheshire)
Halton (Cheshire)
Frodsham
Helsby

Macclesfield
Chesterfield

Mold
Coed Talon
Llanfynydd
Ffrith
Brymbo
Coed Poeth
Berwig
Rhostyllen
Legacy
Rhos

CHESTER
Balderton
Rossett
Gresford (for Llay)
Hightown Halt
Johnstown & Hafod
Marchwiel
Sesswick Halt

WREXHAM
The Lodge
Plas Power
Moss
Acrefair
Ruabon
Rhosymedre
Cefn Halt
Whitehurst Halt
Bangor-on-Dee
Overton-on-Dee
Trench Halt
Fenn's Bank
Bettisfield

CREWE
Willaston
Nantwich
Audlem
Adderley

Stoke
Derby
Burton-on-Trent

Whitchurch (Salop)

Llangollen
Glyndyfrdwy
Carrog
Berwyn
Sun Bank Halt
Trevor
Glyn
Llangollen Line

Gobowen
Park Hall Halt
Oswestry
Llanymynech
Pant (Salop)
Llynclys
Four Crosses
Arddleen
Pool Quay

Whittington H.L.
Whittington L.L.
Frankton
Rednal & West Felton
Baschurch

Welshampton
Ellesmere
Wem

SHREWSBURY
Upton Magna
Walcot
Admaston
Wellington
Hadnall
Leaton

Market Drayton
Tern Hill
Wollerton Halt
Hodnet
Peplow
Ellerdine Halt
Crudgington

Stafford

Welshpool
Forden
Montgomery
Abermule
Newtown
Scafell
Moat Lane Junc

Breidden
Buttington
Plealey Rd
Pontesbury
Minsterley
Leebotwood
Church Stretton
Marsh Brook

Berrington (Severn Val)
Condover
Cressage
Dorrington
Much Wenlock
Presthope
Longville
Rushbury
Harton Road

Ketley
Lawley Bank
Horsehay & Dawley
Buildwas
Iron Br & Broseley
Coalport
Linley

Oakengates
Hadley
Shifnal
Lightmoor
Coalbrookdale
Albrighton
Codsall

Dunstall Park
WOLVERHAMPTON
Wednesfield
Willenhall
Bilston
Priestfield
Bilston
Prince's End
Tipton
Wednesbury
Swan Village
West Bromwich
Handsworth & Smethwick
Soho & Winson Green
Hockley
BIRMINGHAM (Snow Hill)

Lichfield

Craven Arms & Stokesay
Onibury
Bromfield
Ludlow

Ditton Priors
Cleobury North
Burwarton Halt
Aston Botterell Halt
Stottesdon
Prescott Halt
Cleobury Town Halt
Detton Ford Halt

Bridgnorth
Eardington
Hampton Loade
Highley
Arley

Himley
Womborn
Daisy Bank & Bradley
DUDLEY
Blowers Green
Round Oak
Brierley Hill
Brettell Lane

Old Hill
Smethwick
Halesowen
(Moor St.)

Small Heath & Sparkbrook
Tyseley
Acock's Green
Olton
Solihull
Widney Manor
Knowle & Dorridge
Lapworth
Hatton

Stourbridge
Hagley
Churchill & Blakedown
Stourbridge Junc.

Kidderminster
Foley Park
Bewdley
Burlish Halt
Stourport

Easton Court
Tenbury Wells
Newnham Br.
Neen Sollars
Cleobury Mortimer
Wyre Forest

Spring Rd
Hall Green
Yardley Wood
Shirley

Grimes Hill & Wythall
Hartlebury
Earlswood Lakes
Wood End Halt
Danzey (for Tanworth)
Henley-in-Arden

Claverdon
WARWICK
LEAM

Presteign
Forge Crossing Halt
Marston Halt
Kingsland
LEOMINSTER
Berrington & Eye
Woofferton
Stoke Prior Halt
Steens Bridge
Fencote
Rowden Mill
Bromyard

Droitwich Spa
Fernhill Heath
Cutnall Green
Stoke Works

New Radnor
Dolyhir
Stanner
Kington
Titley
Lyonshall
Almeley
Eardisley
Kinnersley
Moorhampton
Credenhill
Ford Bridge
Dinmore
Moreton-on-Lugg
Withington (Hereford)
Suckley
Knightwick
Leigh Court
Newland
Rushwick Halt
Bransford Rd.

WORCESTER (Shrub Hill)
Foregate St.
Henwick
Norton Junction
Stoulton
Pershore
Fladbury

Wotton Wawen Halt
Aston Cantlow
Gt. Alne
Alcester

STRATFORD UPON AVON
Bearley
Wilmcote
Milcote
Long Marston
Honeybourne

Builth Wells
Aberedw

Hay
Clifford
Greens Siding
Westbrook
Whitney
Dorstone
Glasbury
Peterchurch
Vowchurch
Bacton
Abbeydore
St. Devereux
Tram Inn

HEREFORD
Stoke Edith
Asperton
Colwall
Malvern Link
Malvern (Great)
Malvern Wells
Ledbury
Ledbury Town Halt

EVESHAM
Littleton & Badsey
Weston-sub-Edge
Willersey Halt
Broadway (Worcester)
Laverton Halt
Blockley
Toddington
Winchcombe
Gretton Halt
Hayles Abbey Halt
Moreton-in-Marsh

Shipston-on-Stour
Longdon Rd.
Stretton-on-Fosse
Campden

Llandrindod Wells

Holme Lacy
Ballingham
Fawley
Dymock
Newent
Barber's Bridge
Tewkesbury
Bishop's Cleeve
Gotherington
Race Course Stn
(Malvern Rd.)
Churchdown

Three Cocks Junc.
Talgarth
Trefeinon
Llangorse Lake Halt
Talyllyn Junc.
Brecon

Ross
Walford Halt
Kerne Bridge
Lydbrook Junc.
Symonds Y
Mitcheldean Rd.
Drybrook
Longhope

Weston-under-Penyard
Pontrilas

CHELTENHAM SPA (St. James)

Stow-on-the-Wold
Bourton-on-the-Water
Andoversford

Adlestrop
Kingham
Bloxham
Hook Norton
Chipping
Sarsden Ha
Shipton

Pentir Rhiw
Crickhowell
Llanvihangel
Llansantffraed
Pandy

Blaenavon
Moat Lane Junc

Introduction

Passengers from Liverpool travelling through Chester and the Welsh border to Hereford and far beyond could have begun their journeys by sea! GWR timetables showed all departures being from Liverpool Landing Stage with connections at Birkenhead Woodside terminus, 15 minutes later after a short crossing on the Birkenhead ferry.

The Landing Stage was well known as one of the longest floating structures in the world, used by large liners sailing to and from North America but was almost unknown as the official terminus of the Birkenhead Joint Railway. This was the most joint of joint lines: GWR locomotives hauling trains of LMS coaches (including through coaches for Euston) and LMS engines hauling GWR coaches (including Birkenhead-Paddington expresses).

The GWR had booking and parcels offices upgraded to a 'station' in publicity leaflets encouraging overseas tourists to use GWR services as the only ones between Liverpool and London passing through Wales. Passengers could buy tickets from GWR staff who met arriving liners, or from the Landing Stage booking office, where, if gales were blowing and tides were running strongly, they could feel a gentle swell beneath their feet.

Ocean passengers could travel via Birkenhead by five routes: Chester, Shrewsbury and Birmingham direct; the 'Royal Shakespeare' route skirting the Welsh border and passing through either Stratford-upon-Avon or the Severn Valley; or Hereford, Ross and Gloucester; or through Hereford, Bristol and Bath. None, of course, was anything like as quick as catching a nonstop 'Ocean Liner' express to Euston from Riverside station at the foot of the gangway.

Similar journeys are still possible from Liverpool today, either by ferry to Birkenhead (far less frequent than years ago) or Merseyrail Wirral Line EMUs to Chester. Almost all you need to enjoy a view from the past of railways stretching from the Mersey through the Welsh Marches to Hereford and beyond is a current passenger timetable. This is because all the main lines survive.

A remarkably large network, once predominantly Great Western, survived the ravages of Beeching to retain regular passenger services on routes from Birkenhead to Chester, (now third-rail electrified) and south through industrial Wrexham and Ruabon to

Left:
The main stem of the North Wales border railways: Birkenhead-Chester-Shrewsbury-Hereford was linked to main lines, secondary routes and branch lines serving areas far beyond. *Author's collection*

Right:
Birkenhead Woodside, the northern terminus of the Birkenhead Joint. Mogul No 42942 heads the 14.45 Paddington express on New Year's Eve, 1966. This was the last 'Crab' passenger diagram of Birkenhead shed. *Ian Allan Library/N. Matthews*

Left:
Birkenhead Town station at the southern mouth of Woodside Tunnel was closed on 7 May 1945. Thirteen years later, Stanier 2-6-0 No 42977 passes the derelict buildings with an express. *R. W. Miller collection/J. A. Peden*

Right:
A variety of locomotives handled Paddington expresses over the 15 miles between Birkenhead and Chester General station. On 29 May 1966, Stanier 2-6-4 tank No 42613 passes Birkenhead carriage sidings with the 15.25 to Paddington. The tracks on the left led to Birkenhead Docks. *Ian Allan Library/ Brian Taylor*

Shrewsbury. Here, lines radiate south to Hereford, South Wales and Bristol, northeast to Crewe, east to the West Midlands and west to Welshpool on a single track.

Notable long-distance passenger routes have gone: from Paddington to Birkenhead, which once spearheaded broad gauge promoters' hopes of reaching the Mersey; the North to West of England express route via Shrewsbury and Hereford established with the opening of the Severn Tunnel in 1887, and the GWR secondary route between Ruabon and Barmouth which left the Cambrian main line via Welshpool and Machynlleth as the only rail link to the long Cambrian coast route.

They were the most spectacular economies, but the most substantial have been the closure of a host of varied branch lines: long, short, single, mineral, eccentric, unusual and private. It is many years since trails of smoke betrayed the presence of veteran locomotives on remote country branches or in the sidings of collieries, steelworks and quarries.

Recalling memories can be fun, not least through the uncomplicated pleasure of random browsing through magazines. I was reminded of this when I opened the May 1961 issue of *Trains Illustrated*. It reported TUCC approval for

withdrawal of passenger services between Woofferton and Tenbury, but refused immediate consent for similar economy between Tenbury and Kidderminster. On a revivalist note, the second annual meeting of the Welshpool & Llanfair Preservation Company was told of tremendous progress and the early return from Oswestry Works of *The Earl* in good working order.

Acknowledgements

Writing this book has taken me back to places and railways I have known for many years. R. W. (Bob) Miller, my Cambrian and North Staffordshire co-author, kindly read the manuscript and fine-tuned some of my thoughts and provided a number of photographs. Sources I have used include letters from Geoffrey Bannister, who sadly died while this book was being written, Gordon Biddle, Harold Forster MBE, Ken Lucas (archivist of the Bishop's Castle Railway Society), Nigel Payton and Richard Price. Particularly useful were Railtour notes of the Branch Line Society, the Railway Canal & Historical Society and the Wirral Railway Circle.

1. Chester

The first time my parents took me to Chester to see its Roman and medieval remains, I was far more interested in its railways. Nothing was more captivating than watching a veteran GWR 'Saint' class 4-6-0 slowly and majestically rounding the Welsh curve at the north end of General station to enter a bay platform. The faded chocolate and cream of its corridor coaches was almost swamped by khaki for this was a wartime troop train with soldiers leaning out of every window.

They were being posted to a host of Army camps on the city outskirts, among them The Dale where men watched trains on the Birkenhead Joint line as they waited to join assault courses or to shoot on rifle ranges.

The railway scene at Chester was complex and fascinating, it being the hub of main, secondary and local lines of three of the Big

Four post-Grouping companies, the GWR, LMSR and LNER. Earlier, LNWR and GWR main lines had joined at the north end of General station, overlooked by higher ground carrying the Cheshire Lines approach to its own station at Northgate. A triangle just north of the station was completed by its through route from Yorkshire, via Woodhead Tunnel to Birkenhead Docks. The LNER's presence was through takeover of the Great Central Railway and close links with the Cheshire Lines Committee.

Hundreds of miles of railway of two of the Big Four companies were controlled from Chester. Euston dominated, partly because of its influence in northeast Wales, where the GWR had virtually nothing, except around Wrexham.

The territory of the LMS District Traffic

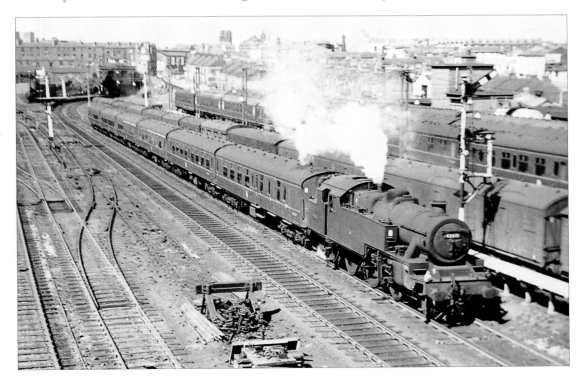

7

Manager at Chester embraced the main line to Holyhead, the Birkenhead Joint and stretched south from Bangor to the windswept junction at Afon Wen, almost 90 rail miles from Chester. South of Chester the LMS area ran to Coalport in Shropshire and included a little-known 15-mile LNWR branch through rural south Cheshire from Tattenhall Junction on the Crewe main line, to Whitchurch. Political in concept, it had been built as the LNWR attempted to break the Shrewsbury & Chester Railway traffic monopoly.

Chester's two main stations were compared in the German-published Baedeker travel guides. Around the turn of the century they noted that General was 'an extensive and handsome building, used in common by the LNWR and GWR', while Northgate was dismissed as a suburban station for the line to Wrexham etc. Yet both were busy enough for hotel omnibuses to meet trains.

The heaviest traffic, passenger and goods, was carried by the Birkenhead Joint with some routed over a west to north curve (still extant) connecting it with the Chester & Holyhead Railway north of Chester General station by which summer relief and excursion traffic could avoid reversal. The spur was perhaps more useful for through freight workings.

General station opened in 1848 and was owned jointly by the LNWR, the Chester & Holyhead, the Birkenhead, Lancashire & Cheshire Junction and the Shrewsbury & Chester, later GWR. It was the culmination of eight years of railway development which began with the opening in September 1840 of the Chester & Birkenhead Railway, which became the BL&CJR in 1847. A few days after the C&BR opened, the Chester & Crewe Railway was completed by the Grand Junction Railway. The next major development was the opening by the C&HR from Chester to Saltney Junction in November 1846.

Following the opening of General station, the C&HR extended with a branch from Saltney to Mold in the summer of 1849. The next year, the BL&CJR was extended from Chester to Walton Junction at Warrington. The Whitchurch branch followed in 1872, but a far more significant development was the northern extension of the Birkenhead Joint from a terminus at Monks' Ferry, Birkenhead, to a spacious terminus at

Left:
The 7pm West Kirby-Birkenhead Woodside headed by GWR 2-6-2 tank No 4124 runs past wooden-platformed Kirby Park station on 7 August 1954. The station had closed a few weeks earlier, ahead of branch passenger services which were withdrawn in autumn 1956.
Ian Allan Library/N. R. Knight

Above right:
Twilight years on the West Kirby branch. The RCTS 'Cheshire Railtour' at Thurstaston in March 1960 – a period between the withdrawal of passenger services and complete branch closure. The station site is now the headquarters of the Wirral Country Park.
Author's collection

Centre right:
A winter 'Welshman' between Euston and North Wales, leaving Chester behind unnamed 'Patriot' No 45513. The express was sometimes run in three portions at summer holiday peaks, all nonstop between Euston and North Wales.
Ian Allan Library/J. D. Mills

Below right:
A classic LMS official photograph of the 'Irish Mail' crossing the Dee Bridge, Chester with 'Royal Scot' No 6166 *London Rifle Brigade*. The dense smoke was probably arranged to give an impression of speed.
Ian Allan Library

Left:
Another of Chester's nonstop express services: a North Staffordshire Potteries' Wake special from Stoke to Llandudno passing Rhyl. The train is likely to have been full, for the date was July 1919 – the first summer after World War 1. The locomotive is a North Staffordshire Railway 4-4-0, specially built for the working. *Author's collection/ Hugh B. Oliver*

Below:
A Birkenhead-Paddington express crossing the River Dee behind 'Castle' class 4-6-0 No 5031 *Totnes Castle* with tender piled high. August 1953. *Ian Allan Library/Kenneth Field*

Birkenhead Woodside, alongside that of the ferry to Liverpool. The Chester-Liverpool direct passenger route over the Birkenhead Joint was some 10 miles shorter than via Runcorn, which, of course, was also used by freight.

Expresses, some of which were completing journeys from Paddington, Euston, the South Coast and North Wales, were allowed about 26 minutes between Chester and Rock Ferry. In just over a quarter of an hour longer, Liverpool passengers could reach Central (Low Level). Stopping train services had overall timings of some 53 minutes by underground, while passengers who enjoyed sea breezes had a 10-minute longer journey by ferry.

The alternative Chester-Liverpool route via Runcorn was lengthy, with stopping trains taking a little over an hour to cover the 27 miles, and semi-fast expresses only about 15 minutes less. Few of the stopping services called at all 12 intermediate stations. Two on the eastern outskirts of Chester – Mickle Trafford and Dunham Hill – warranted only two services a day, although they had two more on the Chester General-Warrington Bank Quay-Manchester Exchange main line, heavily used by Manchester-North Wales expresses. For many years until 1943 some North Wales expresses were worked by GWR locomotives between Manchester Exchange and Chester because the Warrington-Chester section was a joint line.

The most prestigious of Chester's passenger services were the day and night Euston-Holyhead 'Irish Mails' and the Paddington-Birkenhead GWR expresses. These trains ran in and out of Chester General station in opposite directions and occasionally the up Mails and the up Paddingtons passed each other between

Below:
'Jubilee' class 4-6-0 No 45606 *Falkland Islands* with a fitted freight for North Wales; the spur (left) links the Chester & Holyhead with the Birkenhead route. The now-demolished GWR shed is behind the signal gantry (right).
Ian Allan Library/John S. Whiteley

there and Saltney Junction. While the LNWR took passengers to Chester in four hours from Euston after a 179-mile journey, GWR departures from Paddington took about 50 minutes longer over a route of an extra 16 miles.

The LMS and GWR both published guide books to their routes via Chester. *LMS Route Book Number One*, covering Euston-Holyhead journeys, included a graphic description of departure from Chester: 'The train gathers speed rapidly as if the locomotive had a horse sense of the last lap of its journey and strained towards the mountain airs of Snowdon.' Such purple prose was contained in only the first edition published in the late 1930s. It was deleted when a revised route book was published shortly before Nationalisation – possibly to discourage drivers making too lively a start from Chester.

The GWR Paddington to Birkenhead guide was prosaic, its mood being established by its subtitle: *200 miles of English and Welsh Country as seen from the GWR Trains.* Holiday – as opposed to route – guides were a family favourite for many years, avidly read by mums and dads sitting by the fireside on long winter evenings. They led to a constant growth of another of Chester's railway attractions: holiday specials working to and from the North Wales coast. Traffic reached its peak on summer Saturdays and, as D. S. M. Barrie reminded

readers of Ian Allan's *Trains Annual* of 1955, this traffic was some of the most intensive of its kind run on the railways of Britain. It included specials to and from the Butlin's holiday camp at Pwllheli over the LMS route via Bangor. The camp was also reached by GWR trains from Birkenhead, which reversed at Chester to go forward via Ruabon, Barmouth and the Cambrian line.

There is a point midway between Criccieth and Portmadoc which is the same distance from Chester and Birkenhead by the LMS and GWR routes.

Holiday traffic developed over many years and railway companies were quick to exploit its potential. The North Staffordshire Railway, which regarded the North Wales coast as being on its holiday doorstep, went so far as to build a small class of 4-4-0 tender locomotives for return workings between Stoke and Llandudno. The specials ran only in summer and the traffic was small in comparison with business expresses between Llandudno and Manchester, which included club trains for wealthy businessmen who loved to live by the sea and

Right:
Strong shadows give a striking atmosphere to Chester General station on summer evenings — a scene captured after the arrival of a train of compartment coaches headed by Class 2 4-4-0 No 40653. *Kenneth Field*

Below:
A Birkenhead-Paddington departing Chester behind No 1008 *County of Cardigan* in filthy condition in the early 1950s after part of the roof had been removed. The long footbridge in the background linked the Hoole district with the station and city centre. It was used by hundreds of local residents each day despite the 1d toll. *Ian Allan Library/ E. N. Kneale*

Above:
Waverton, the first wayside station south of Chester on the Crewe main line, was sometimes shunted by large locomotives. Crosti-boilered 9F class 2-10-0 No 92029 dominates its surroundings. *H. Forster*

Left:
A post-Grouping wanderer: an Aspinall 0-6-0 at Chester in 1923 still carrying its L&Y No 105. *Ian Allan Library*

who often had their own seats in first class coaches. As late as the 1950s, I was told, a replacement coach had had to be turned on Llandudno turntable because its regular passengers wanted their individual seats on the seaward side of the main line.

Chester was the main hub of several LNWR branches, notable for carrying long distance stopping services. Made up of compartment coaches and hauled by veteran LNWR locomotives – tank and tender – some took 2hr 30min for the journey, calling at more than 20 wayside stations in the 48 miles between Chester, Mold, Denbigh and Corwen. By changing at Denbigh a tourist with time to spare could travel leisurely between Chester and Rhyl through the Vale of Clwyd instead of using the Chester & Holyhead main line.

Below:
An eastbound goods departs from Saltney Junction on 11 August 1962 hauled by Class 8F No 48693. The second locomotive is GWR pannier tank No 8784 en route from Wrexham to Crewe for scrapping. *Ian Allan Library/Derek Cross*

Another alternative route from Chester to Rhyl, possibly never used by passengers, was from Northgate station using a Wrexham service to Connah's Quay, where a cinder path and wooden steps linked LNER High Level with the C&HR station where a main line stopper could be caught. It was also possible for passengers to vary routes by changing from LMS and LNER local trains at Hope Exchange.

LMS Chester-based locomotives were workhorses – often veteran LNWR survivors in the 1940s, for it was home to the 'bin-ends' of 'Precursor' and 'George the Fifth' class 4-4-0s, which I watched with delight in full hue and cry along the North Wales coast. Even on all-station stoppers, they had a dignity and appeal of their own.

Paddington Presence

The Chester Division of the GWR extended for 382 route miles and 633 track miles stretching from Wolverhampton (Stafford Road) to Birkenhead and Warrington. It included some 20 miles over the LMS between Warrington (Walton New Junction) and Manchester,

exercising running powers. Running powers were also claimed over the LMS between Crewe and Manchester, but were never used.

The first revenue paid by the GWR to the LNWR was for running powers over the Chester & Holyhead from Saltney to a junction with the Birkenhead Joint, 1¼ miles away in one of the approach tunnels to General station. The GWR paid for running powers from Saltney to the Birkenhead Joint until Nationalisation, using the southern two tracks of the quadrupled section.

Saltney was the hub of GWR Chester freight traffic, which was heavier than that of the LNWR which marshalled at Crewe, Warrington and also, like the GWR, at Birkenhead Docks. Saltney marshalling yard, just south of the junction with the Holyhead main line, was active virtually round the clock with three shunting engines rostered to work 300 hours a week. Only between midday and midnight on Sundays did hush descend on this boundary area of England and Wales. For the rest of the week the yard handled some 90 arriving and departing trains and 1,200 wagons – rather less

than the total for which it was designed. Workings included trips to GWR Brook Lane depot near the General station, which handled some Warrington and Manchester freight until after Grouping, when Saltney yard was enlarged, enabling staff economies to be made at Brook Lane.

One of Saltney's shunting engines ran through the yard to join a short single-line branch serving a small shipbuilding yard, two manure works, a wire manufacturing works and a short wharf on a tidal section of the River Dee. The class 1 yardmaster had a staff of about 70 men, half of whom were goods guards. There were also three junior telephone attendants.

The branch level crossing over the former A55 road (now A5104) is the border between England and Wales.

Below:
A Royal train carrying HRH Princess Margaret returning from Chester to London passes Waverton on 28 May 1954. Rebuilt 'Patriot' No 45523 *Bangor* has an ordinary express headcode. *H. Forster*

Right:
GWR ex-ROD 2-8-0s worked on the Shrewsbury & Chester for many years, some being stationed at Chester. No 3016 clears Saltney Junction with a train of mixed mineral wagons. Chester & Holyhead trains used the two northern tracks in the background. *Ian Allan Library/S. D. Wainwright*

Below:
Perhaps the most unusual of passenger trains calling at remote rural stations in south Cheshire was an early afternoon working between Chester and Whitchurch. On Wednesdays it carried through coaches between Chester and Shrewsbury, but there was no similar return working. A classic W. A. Camwell study of 1955 with a Whitchurch-bound local headed by 4-4-0 No 40413. The service was withdrawn two years later, although the route continued for locomotive testing and diversions for some time afterwards. *Author's collection/ W. A. Camwell*

Left:
Pannier tank No 4683 approaches Hawarden Bridge with the 09.16 New Brighton-Wrexham Central on 30 August 1965 – five years after the northern terminal of the service had been switched from Seacombe to New Brighton. *G. F. A. Hobbs*

Centre left:
The North Wales & Liverpool Railway, running from Hawarden Bridge to the Wirral Railway at Bidston, became part of the Great Central soon after opening. Excursion traffic was popular for Merseysiders wanting to enjoy the countryside and hills north of Wrexham. *Author's collection*

Below left:
From Connah's Quay, the Wrexham, Mold & Connah's Quay route climbed sharply from the platform end towards Hawarden. The Chester & Wirral platform had the main offices with brick chimneys in the timber building. *Ian Allan Library*

Right:
After arrival at Hooton South Junction from Chester, '8F' class 2-8-0 No 48749 prepares to propel its tankers to the Gulf oil refinery at Ellesmere Port on 14 June 1963. The single-track West Kirby branch went off to the right. *Ian Allan Library/D. Ian Wood*

NORTH WALES and LIVERPOOL RAILWAY.

HALF-HOLIDAY EXCURSIONS TO NORTH WALES.

Every Monday, Thursday, Saturday and Sunday,

UNTIL FURTHER NOTICE, DEAN & DAWSON'S CHEAP DAY AND HALF-DAY EXCURSION TICKETS WILL BE ISSUED TO

CONNAH'S QUAY and SHOTTON,

HAWARDEN,

BUCKLEY JUNCTION,

CAERGWRLE CASTLE (for HOPE MOUNTAIN), WREXHAM and ELLESMERE,

AS UNDER:

Passengers return the same day by any Ordinary Train having a Through Connection.

Saturdays excepted.   *No Bookings to Ellesmere on Sundays.*

BY ORDER.

DEAN & DAWSON, 23, Water Street, LIVERPOOL.

South of Saltney, where the station was a wartime casualty in 1916, there were three country stations before Wrexham, the first, Balderton having a two-mile narrow gauge railway linking the station yard with Eaton Hall, seat of the Dukes of Westminster. Rossett handled strawberry specials to Liverpool and Manchester during the annual season, as well as agricultural produce the year round.

Gresford Halt, on the northern outskirts of Wrexham, suffered competition from road transport and from a village station on the Great Central line to Hawarden Bridge and Chester.

As part of the Birkenhead Joint, Chester General station was controlled by the joint superintendent at Shrewsbury, but most of the 56-mile joint line was within the Wirral Peninsula. Its main branch – but least important – was the 12½-mile line from Hooton to West Kirby.

A happy memory of boyhood is walking the shore of the Dee Estuary near West Kirby and watching the distant trails of smoke from expresses pounding a fast stretch of the Chester & Holyhead main line back-clothed by the Welsh hills. Occasionally, the distant rumble of the expresses would be drowned by the more vociferous bark of a GWR 2-6-2 tank, far too powerful for its four compartment coaches, sedately hauling a local train on the Hooton-West Kirby single-track behind me.

The branch finally closed in 1962, after which it carved a niche in environmental history as one of the first trackbeds to be converted into a country park. On a sunny day it is enjoyed by hundreds of walkers who far outnumber the passengers who knew it as a route to be avoided whenever possible, being far too roundabout a journey between small towns and villages.

The branch was nearly 60 years old at Grouping, having been built from Hooton to Parkgate, a small town beside the Dee, in 1866 and extended north along the low cliffs of the estuary to West Kirby 20 years later. It pierced a land of large estates of shipping magnates who began and ended their journeys to and from Birkenhead in their own club car attached to trains they considered convenient.

Branch services were included in three major timetables: one by each of the joint-owning companies and the third in Bradshaw's in which, in late Victorian days, services were classed as '1 & 2 gov'. The branch timetable

was 'buried' by Bradshaw's in a widely ranging table embracing Manchester, Warrington, Frodsham, Chester, Parkgate, Birkenhead and Liverpool. A junction with the Wirral Railway was opened at West Kirby, but hopes of developing through passenger services never came to fruition.

A ponderous footnote in LNWR public timetables advised passengers that through tickets to and from the Wirral Railway did not include the cost of conveyance between the termini. It stated that they travelled between them at their own expense but, in fact, the stations could hardly have been closer, being separated only by a small coal and goods yard.

It was only in the 1930s that through trains used the junction between the lines – a through coach service between New Brighton and Euston – which was abandoned on the outbreak of World War 2. Two corridor coaches sandwiched between ex-LNWR compartment stock gave a 'high and mighty' importance to the local sets into which they were marshalled.

The creation of Wirral Country Park, better known locally as the Wirral Way, included the restoration of Hadlow Road station – which served the affluent village of Willaston – as a time-warped village station of the 1950s. The headquarters of the park are at Thurstaston on a site landscaped over wartime concrete anti-aircraft gun emplacements too strong to be demolished by explosives.

Cheshire Lines Committee

The joke about a schoolboy who wrote that a Roman soldier never lived to be a centurion was also true of the Cheshire Lines Committee's presence at Chester, for Manchester, Sheffield & Lincolnshire Railway's and CLC passenger services, begun as late as 1874, lasted only until 1969.

While much of Chester's rail network has survived, losing no more than a few local stations, that of the Cheshire Lines has been virtually obliterated. The draughty barn-like Northgate station, close to the city walls, was ugly but had the merit of being handy for the city centre, unlike the more distantly sited General station. For many years the largest sign, which stretched across its two wide platforms, directed passengers to the refreshment and tea room, rather than trains, of which there were plenty to Wrexham Central, via Connah's Quay (until September 1968) and Manchester Central. Both duplicated through routes, but were far more local in character. Northgate-Manchester Central services were switched to Chester General station in October 1969 and to Manchester Piccadilly via Stockport

Left:
The quiet midday scene at Chester Northgate with a two-coach DMU waiting to depart with the 12.35 to Wrexham on 16 June 1967. *S. Creer*

rather than over the former Manchester South Junction & Altrincham, which is now part of the Manchester Metrolink tramway.

Northgate was a legacy of the CLC's ambiguous attitude towards Chester, which could be detected from its entry in annual editions of the *Railway Year Book*. It placed Chester last in the list of large stations and last but one among the principal towns it served, below much smaller ones including Northwich and Winsford.

Half a mile from Northgate was Liverpool Road station which had four platforms up to closure in 1951, although Wrexham trains used only two. The others were on a through route between Yorkshire and North Wales, opened when the Great Central, as the MS&LR had become three years earlier, extended westwards to Hawarden in 1890. The route never carried regular passenger services.

My CLC memories are strong because they date from the impressionable years of youth in the early 1940s when Northgate avoiding line was used by long and heavy freight trains carrying war weapons for export from Birkenhead Docks. At their head were Robinson 2-8-0s whose often near-empty tenders were replenished at Bidston shed, where the shed master was Campbell Highet, who became a railway author of note. He always welcomed visitors whose interest in railways extended beyond spotting.

Northgate and Liverpool Road stations at Chester were connected by a sharp and heavily graded curve, often troublesome to small tank locomotives in bad weather. Both curves leading into Northgate from the Wrexham and Manchester lines had 15mph speed restrictions.

The Wrexham route had several ornate but little-used stations on the outskirts of Chester, but once across the Dee at Hawarden Bridge, it was well used by local passengers travelling to Wrexham, notably shoppers.

When easterly winds blew, Northgate was occasionally shrouded by smoke from locomotives on the adjacent CLC two-road shed used by veteran locomotives working local passenger and goods services. But it was not CLC smoke because the joint company never owned its own locomotives, only sheds. Locomotives, which gave four short whistles when moving on and off shed, shunted the goods and coal yard and also a single siding which crossed the Chester & Holyhead main line to reach a banana warehouse.

The Northgate avoiding line was once part of one of the most roundabout holiday routes in railway history. The Great Central worked it from the East Midlands to the Cambrian coast, via Woodhead, Chester, Wrexham, Ellesmere and Oswestry.

Right:
Chester Northgate terminal was a functional barn in contrast to the stylish General station, but for years it was busy and popular with its passengers for it was close to the city centre, just beyond the city walls. On 29 September 1949, a Robinson Class C13 4-4-2 tank, No 67433, awaits departure with the 4.15pm Cheshire Lines service to Manchester Central.
Author's collection

BRITISH RAILWAYS

IMPROVED
SLEEPING CAR
SERVICE

BIRKENHEAD — LONDON
(WOODSIDE)   (PADDINGTON)

LEAVING BIRKENHEAD 1 HOUR 40 MINUTES LATER

Commencing 13th June 1955, the FIRST and THIRD CLASS SLEEPING CAR
advertised on the 7.15 p.m. Birkenhead (Woodside) to London (Paddington) will
leave Birkenhead (Woodside) at 8.55 p.m., arriving London (Paddington) at 5.10 a.m.

PRINCIPAL STATIONS SERVED—						Monday to Saturday Nights	
Birkenhead (Woodside)	..	..	..	..	..	dep.	8.55 p.m.
Chester (General)	..	..	..	..	..	dep.	9.45 p.m.
Wrexham General	..	..	..	..	..	dep.	10. 7 p.m.
Ruabon	..	..	..	..	..	dep.	10.18 p.m.
Gobowen	..	..	..	..	..	dep.	10.32 p.m.
Shrewsbury	..	..	..	..	..	dep.	11.10 p.m.
Wellington	..	..	..	..	..	dep.	11.30 p.m.
Wolverhampton (Low Level)	..	..	..	..	..	dep.	12.20 a.m.
Birmingham (Snow Hill)	..	..	..	..	..	{ arr.	12.40 a.m.
						{ dep.	1. 0 a.m.
Paddington	..	..	..	..	..	arr.	5.10 a.m.

On arrival at Paddington, passengers may remain in the sleeping car until 8.0 a.m.
The facility is available to passengers joining or alighting at any intermediate station at which
this train calls.

The First and Third Class Sleeping Car will continue to be conveyed on the 12.5 a.m.
PADDINGTON to BIRKENHEAD (Woodside) on Monday to Saturday mornings
inclusive as already advertised

SLEEPING BERTH CHARGES

1st Class, 27s. 0d. per person in addition to the 1st Class Fare
3rd Class, 11s. 0d. per person in addition to the 3rd Class Fare

Application for Berths specifying class, number required and whether for Lady or Gentleman, or
for both, should be made to :—
STATION MASTER'S OFFICE, PADDINGTON.
DISTRICT OPERATING SUPERINTENDENT, CHESTER.
or to any Station.

Full details may be obtained from Stations, Offices and Agencies.

Printed in England by Joseph Wones Ltd., West Bromwich ; also at Birmingham and London.

Left:
A 1955 speed-up of the Birkenhead-Paddington sleeping car service by nearly two hours was achieved without cancelling stops at Hooton, Chester, Wrexham, Ruabon and Gobowen. It was introduced a fortnight later than intended and survived for 12 more years until being withdrawn at the same time as the day expresses, from 6 March 1967. *Author's collection*

Below left:
The 10.28am departure from Kirby Park on 20 August 1934 saw the guard collect the Joyce station clock being sent to the makers at Whitchurch for repair. The waybill instructed the guard to see that entries on the bill corresponded with parcels delivered to him. *Author's collection*

Right:
An Easter 1933 day excursion from south Cheshire rural stations to North Wales saw trains departing over a three-hour period from breakfast-time. Passengers who caught a Chester departure shortly before midday would have had only a short time at the furthest destination of Llandudno. *Author's collection*

Below left:
Diesel services between Wrexham Central, Chester Northgate and New Brighton in the timetable from September 1960 were far more intensive than steam services had been but, despite that, they were not successful. *Author's collection*

Below right:
Cheap day returns from both Chester stations to a dozen local ones again failed to attract many passengers despite the slogan on handbills 'travel in rail comfort'. *Author's collection*

EASTER EXCURSIONS, 1933.
A DAY IN NORTH WALES.
EASTER MONDAY, APRIL 17th,
EXCURSION TICKETS TO
Prestatyn, Rhyl, Colwyn Bay and Llandudno

FROM	Times of Starting.			RETURN FARES—THIRD CLASS.			
	A	B	C	To Prestatyn.	To Rhyl.	To Colwyn Bay.	To Llandudno.
	a.m.	a.m.	a.m.	s. d.	s. d.	s. d.	s. d.
Worleston	8 16		11 16	4 6	5 0	6 0	7 0
Calveley	8 23		11 23	4 0	4 6	5 6	6 6
Beeston Castle & Tarporley	8 29		11 29	4 0	4 6	5 6	6 6
Tattenhall Road	8 37		11 36	3 6	4 0	5 0	6 0
Waverton	8 43	9 29	11† 0	3 0	3 6	4 6	5 6
Whitchurch		8 53	10†30	5 0	5 0	6 0	7 0
Malpas		9 4	10†41	4 0	4 6	5 6	6 6
Broxton		9 13	10†47	4 0	4 0	5 0	6 0
Tattenhall		9 19	10†52	3 6	4 0	5 0	5 6

A—Passengers change at Chester into train leaving at 9.2 a.m.
B—Change at Chester and proceed by special train at 9.45 a.m.
C—Change at Chester and proceed by special train at 12.5 p.m.
†—Passengers change at Chester into train leaving at 11.45 a.m.

RETURN ARRANGEMENTS—Passengers return the same day as under :—
For Stations Waverton to Worleston—Llandudno 5.40 or 7.30 p.m., Colwyn Bay 6.5 or 7.55 p.m., Rhyl 6.25 or 8.15 p.m., Prestatyn 6.34 or 8.24 p.m.
D—For stations Tattenhall to Whitchurch—Llandudno 6.55 p.m., Colwyn Bay 7.17 p.m., Rhyl 7.39 p.m., Prestatyn 7.52 p.m.

D—9.10 p.m. Chester to Whitchurch, will run specially on this date.

Children under 3 years of age free ; 3 and under 14 half fares.

LUGGAGE ALLOWANCE.
Passengers holding Day or Half-Day Excursion Tickets are not allowed to take any luggage except small handbags, luncheon baskets, or other small articles intended for the passenger's use during the day. On the return journey only, passengers may take with them, free of charge, at Owner's Risk, goods for their own use, not exceeding 60 lbs.

Conditions of Issue of Excursion and other Reduced Fare Tickets.
Excursion Tickets, and Tickets issued at Fares less than the Ordinary Fares, are issued subject to the Notices and Conditions shewn in the Company's current Time Tables.

Further information can be obtained on application to F. P. KINSMAN, District Goods and Passenger Manager, CHESTER. 'Phone Chester 1080—Extension 17.

March, 1933. (Ex/Easter/G) **ASHTON DAVIES, Chief Commercial Manager.**
(E.R.O. 53302.)

(2,500) M℃orquodale & Co., Ltd., Printers, London and Newton.—651 K 115

DIESEL
SERVICES

between

WREXHAM CENTRAL
CHESTER NORTHGATE
and
NEW BRIGHTON

12th SEPTEMBER, 1960, to 11th JUNE, 1961
or until further notice

BRITISH RAILWAYS

PLEASE RETAIN THIS BILL FOR REFERENCE

CHEAP RETURN TICKETS
DAILY BY ANY TRAIN
SUNDAYS WHERE SERVICE PERMITS

1st FEBRUARY 1958
UNTIL FURTHER NOTICE
FROM
CHESTER
GENERAL AND NORTHGATE

BLACON CAPENHURST ELLESMERE PORT HELSBY INCE & ELTON
LEDSHAM LITTLE SUTTON MOLLINGTON MOULDSWORTH SEALAND
STANLOW & THORNTON UPTON-BY-CHESTER
RETURN ON DAY OF ISSUE ONLY

PASSENGERS MAY TERMINATE THE OUTWARD JOURNEY AT ANY INTERMEDIATE STATION ON SURRENDER OF THE OUTWARD HALF OF THE TICKET AND MAY RETURN FROM ANY INTERMEDIATE STATION.

TRAVEL IN RAIL COMFORT

BRITISH RAILWAYS

Left:
Tickets for GWR spring and early summer holidays at 1d a mile in 1932 could be bought from travel agents as well as stations. One source was a GWR booking office in central Liverpool – in an office building opposite James Street underground station. The building was later destroyed in an air raid.
Author's collection

Below left:
Cheshire Lines Committee single from Chester Northgate to Upton for a bicycle, perambulator or child's mail cart, clearly stating 'for one article only'. An early Edwardian issue dated 7 May 1902.

Below right:
LNER monthly return: Chester Northgate to Hawarden Bridge Halt. Undated.

Right:
Wrexham General – on a date unknown, although the women's dress would suggest the 1920s. A loaded coal train is about to depart. A GWR 'no spitting' notice hangs above the ticket collector's booth.
Author's collection

2. Wrexham-Ruabon-Shrewsbury

While Chester grew into a junction of several main lines, Wrexham, and to a lesser degree, Ruabon, five miles to the south, became hubs of the North Wales coalfield webbed by a mass of short, sharply curved and graded single-line branches serving collieries and steelworks.

All have long passed into memory, but Wrexham, by far the largest Welsh town outside the South Wales valleys, and Ruabon, have retained what was historically their own main line, the Shrewsbury & Chester, although today it is reduced to a secondary route.

Pre-Grouping, the Wrexham area was also served by the Great Central (from Chester and the Liverpool-Wallasey passenger ferry at Seacombe & Egremont); the Cambrian Railways from Ellesmere and the GWR/LNWR Joint three-mile Wrexham & Minera Extension Railway. This was a single-line link between Brymbo and the LNWR near the village of Coed Talon, opened from near Mold by the LNWR in 1872.

But none of these lines challenged the dominance of the Great Western, and undisputedly, the largest station was Wrexham General. Alongside, to the west, is Wrexham Exchange, which the Wrexham, Mold & Connah's Quay Railway established before it was taken over by the Great Central. There was no direct connection to allow through running and passengers on occasional through services had to de-train and walk between stations while coaches negotiated the exchange siding, as it was termed. GC trains continued from Exchange, running under the S&C main line to reach Wrexham Central in the busy town centre.

Between 1889 and 1917, Central and Exchange stations handled frequent weekday services on the Great Central's former Wrexham, Mold & Connah's Quay branch to Brymbo. These were run in competition with the GWR's Brymbo branch which had a better-sited terminal by the steelworks. Despite heavy gradients, Bradshaw's noted that the GC operated railmotor cars 'with the exception of Saturdays after 2 aft' when steam trains provided extra services, including late night workings.

The Cambrian worked the Wrexham & Ellesmere Railway from its opening in 1895 until Grouping, after which the GWR

Left:
An evocative reminder of the Brymbo rail scene, with the Minera branch curving sharply as it climbs away from the village. Pannier tank No 9610 is seen with a lightly loaded train for Minera Quarry on 1 June 1966.
Ian Allan Library/A. J. Clarke

Below:
A Manning, Wardle 0-6-0 saddle tank, *Henrietta*, on the steeply graded branch leading to Minera lead mines, c1890.
Clwyd Record Office

Right:
Pannier tank No 9610 on the Minera daily branch goods, 7 May 1966, in pristine condition after being cleaned by enthusiasts from the Birmingham area.
Ian Allan Library/ David Gouldthorp

introduced auto trains. They ran until the branch closed in autumn 1962.

Until the population grew, GWR branches in the Wrexham area were used only by coal and mineral trains. Wrexham-Brymbo services were introduced in 1889, to Coed Talon from Brymbo in 1897 and to Berwig eight years later. Moss Valley services were also started in 1905, with railmotors, which also worked to Coed Poeth and Berwig, Ponkey Crossing Halt, Rhos and Wynn Hall.

In the 1920s, the GWR employed a staff of more than 70 at Wrexham led by a special grade stationmaster. The largest group were 20 signalmen manning nine boxes, the rest included a shunting horse driver and a slipper lad, but not locomotive men, who were based at Croes Newydd shed.

There was a mass of sidings in the Wrexham area owned by railway companies and private coal mines. The biggest group, at Wheatsheaf, could store up to 200 wagons but some sidings, including those for horse boxes, could accommodate only a single van.

Journeys over the Shrewsbury & Chester and the Great Central line to Bidston still hint at the flavour of Wrexham's railways in their heyday, but the branches have been obliterated, the

demolition of railways and collieries being part of one of the most extensive landscaping schemes carried out in Wales. Only isolated remains are left.

Wrexham and Ruabon were industrial areas which presented a challenge to the railway enthusiast for their veritable webs of lines were largely inaccessible to all but the footslogger before the age of the car. Access improved as electric trams and buses, run by small companies, were increasingly successful against rail competition. Partially realising the superiority and advantages of bus operation, the GWR introduced its own services, notably between Wrexham and Brymbo and by 1924, reported that 'a good business is also developing with parties, particularly football, hockey etc clubs at weekends'.

The Ruabon area on the northern lip of the Dee Valley had a number of short branches, some developed privately by local firms. Typical was the Plas Madoc branch, which although GWR owned, was worked by a small shunting tank belonging to Wynnstay Colliery, one of the largest pits in the district. In 1914, nearly 1,400 men were employed, all but about 150 working underground.

Besides the S&C main line, Wrexham and

Ruabon were linked by the Rhos branch, the single line running some three miles from the main line south of Wrexham to Rhos which had a large mining community. The line continued south to terminate in the goods yard at Trevor station on the Llangollen line and at Pontcysyllte canal basin at the northern end of the aqueduct.

The branch had a passenger service for only a comparatively short time – from 1905 to 1931 – but Saturday soccer specials for Wrexham home matches continued for almost as long again, not being withdrawn until the mid-1950s.

Ruabon

Ruabon's importance as the only major junction between Chester and Shrewsbury developed with the progressive push west of a 53-mile GWR secondary route through the Dee Valley to the Cambrian coast at Barmouth Junction, at the south end of the Cambrian's long viaduct across the Mawddach Estuary. The route was begun in 1861 when Llangollen was reached, and completed in 1869. The Ruabon-Llangollen line was doubled in 1898. By then, traffic through Ruabon had increased with the opening in 1882 of the 25-mile branch over the

Arenig mountains between Bala and Blaenau Festiniog (as it was then spelt). It might have gone further had the LNWR exercised running powers it held between Llangollen and Dolgelley, but it never did so.

In its heyday, Ruabon was staffed by over 60 men under a stationmaster designated special class, like his colleague at Wrexham. This staff included 12 men manning five signalboxes, and there were 30 sidings which could handle more than 700 wagons. The station was busy enough with passengers making connections to and from the Dee Valley for the GWR-managed refreshment rooms on both main line platforms to be kept open for more than half the day: from 8.30am until 10pm.

For many customers these were welcome breaks in often long and slow journeys between the coast and Paddington and Birkenhead (for the coast was especially popular with Merseysiders). Others reached Ruabon on connecting LNWR and Lancashire & Yorkshire services from Leeds and Normanton via Manchester Exchange. These services were considered important enough to be shown as whole-page timetables by the GWR.

Not shown were daily mail trains between Chester and Dolgelley, for which the General

Left:
An historic locomotive for an historic train. The 1957 Festiniog Railway Society members' special approaching Ruabon behind No 3440 *City of Truro* on 30 March. *Ian Allan Library/T. E. Williams*

Above right:
A study of the Welsh railway scene; always a delight to rediscover, if only as a reminder of the Llangollen Railway of today. *Leicester Museums*

Centre right:
A Minera branch goods approaching the village on its return to Croes Newydd with pannier tank No 9639 on 8 May 1965. *G. F. A. Hobbs*

Below right:
Wrexham Central looking west towards the Shrewsbury and Chester main line. Class N5 0-6-2 tank No 69349 is with a stopping service from Chester Northgate on 12 August 1950. *Stephenson Locomotive Society/ T. J. Edgington*

Left:
One of the stiffest climbs on the GWR main line north of Shrewsbury was Gresford Bank a few miles north of Wrexham, with gradients rising to 1 in 82. In 1963, 'Hall' class 4-6-0 No 6957 *Norcliffe Hall* climbs with a Paddington-bound express.
Ian Allan Library/R. Hewitt

Centre left:
An excursion composed of compartment stock and headed by 2-6-4 tank No 42493 climbs through Gresford Halt on Easter Monday 1960. The halt served a busy mining area before closure in 1962. It was unmanned for the last seven years.
Ian Allan Library/ Michael Mensing

Below left:
A heavy freight climbs Gresford Bank on 13 August 1955 headed by GWR 2-8-0 No 2871. Unusually, for this class, it is working with a 4,000-gallon tender.
Ian Allan Library/ S. D. Wainwright

Right:
A six-coach chocolate and cream set forms the 2.35pm Birkenhead-Paddington behind 'County' class 4-6-0 No 1017 *County of Hereford* passing the site of Rhos Robin Halt (1932-47) between Gresford and Wrexham on 18 April 1960.
Ian Allan Library/ Michael Mensing

Post Office paid. The 3.5am down and 7.45pm up Sunday workings ceased during World War 1, but until then, the driver of the Sunday morning mail was told he must pass through Llandderfel at 2mph to put out two mail bags from Corwen.

The Dee Valley services were ridiculed for many years. In his book, *A Wayfarer in Wales*, published in 1930, W. Watkin Davies noted: 'No great saving of time will be effected by putting up with such discomfort and travelling by express, for expresses between Ruabon and Barmouth (except, I suppose, to the official eye) are indistinguishable from ordinary trains. Indeed, I have heard it said by the flippant that the only difference between a GWR express and a slow train in Wales is that the latter stops at all stations, while the former stops between all stations!'

Not all expresses called at Ruabon. The daily 9.25am from Birkenhead Woodside to Dover Harbour called at Wrexham at 10.23am and then ran nonstop to Shrewsbury, being allowed 47 minutes for the 25 miles. In the summer of 1905, a prominent footnote reminded passengers that those bound for the Continent would have a 'convenient rest of a few hours at Dover'.

GWR internal reports reflected the social order of the period, listing the principal residents of various districts. The Ruabon list was headed by Sir Watkin Williams Wynn who lived in the family's ancestral home, Wynnstay Hall. He had the right to stop any train to pick up or set down passengers at Ruabon, where during the hunting season, a combined saloon and hounds van and a horse box were stabled for his use. They were serviced and stored at Saltney.

Ruabon-Shrewsbury

In the 25 rail miles separating Ruabon and Shrewsbury there were 13 intermediate stops – eight stations, including Gobowen (junction for Oswestry) and five halts – and two magnificent viaducts.

This was the most fascinating stretch of the Shrewsbury & Chester and provided the greatest challenge to the builders, mainly in the four miles south from Ruabon to Chirk, as the author of Black's *Picturesque Guide to North Wales* wrote in 1869:

'The vale of the Ceiriog at Chirk and the vale of the Dee between Chirk and Llangollen, are distinguished by four notable specimens of engineering and architectural skill – each of these deep valleys being crossed by the Ellesmere Canal and by the Chester & Shrewsbury Railway, upon long ranges of arches at a great elevation.

'The two former are the productions of the late eminent engineer, Mr Telford; and the two latter, of Mr Henry Robertson, the able engineer of the railway company.

'The two aqueducts have long been the objects of general admiration, but they are now surpassed in massive grandeur and importance, by the works of the railway.'

Chirk had another attraction for the enthusiast, the six-mile Glyn Valley Tramway, which for almost 60 years, between 1874 and its closure in 1933, carried passengers. It was busy enough to have its eight weekday services shown in its own timetable within the GWR passenger timetables, although connections between the main line and tramway were not advertised.

The tramway company tried to sell itself to the GWR although nothing came of it and after closure its records were pulped during World War 2, but its history has since been well documented.

Grouping brought changes. The effect of Paddington's takeover of the Cambrian was felt at Whittington, where supervision of the High Level station on the Oswestry, Ellesmere & Whitchurch passed to the stationmaster at Low Level.

At Baschurch, there was concern among local GWR officials that competition might develop with the Shropshire & Montgomeryshire for traffic in the Kinnerley area, even though the lines were separated by several miles.

In recent years, Gobowen station has been carefully restored although it no longer has three ladies' waiting rooms and is no longer a junction, having lost this status when the motor train service over the 2½-mile branch to Oswestry was withdrawn in November 1966.

The S&C route that survives today assumed its shape in autumn 1960 when in a sweeping cull, 15 of the 19 stations and halts were closed leaving only Wrexham General, Ruabon, Chirk and Gobowen served by DMUs. These take some 44 minutes for the journey – about half the time of all-station steam-hauled trains. The economies came after the British Transport Commission found that some halts were used only by a single passenger a day. At Grouping it had a stationmaster, responsible for the ¾-mile Fron branch running from the down loop to Chirk Castle Lime Works. This was worked as part of the main line under an agreement of March 1845, signed ahead of the main line opening between 1846 and 1848.

For years, the S&C carried heavy freight traffic, much of it from the West Midlands bound for Birkenhead Docks. Shunting for through goods trains was carried out at Castle Foregate, Shrewsbury, where the S&C branched away from Shrewsbury's other main lines. This yard had a capacity for 300 wagons and traffic was mainly cattle, timber and minerals.

Left:
Chirk, a village where the GWR revenue about the time of Grouping was some seven times greater for parcels and goods traffic than for passengers. An empty platform scene in 1971 with a DMU on the Chester-Wolverhampton service.
Ian Allan Library/G. Holt

Above right:
'It did not even succeed in reaching man's traditional three score and ten years' – the valediction on the Glyn Valley Tramway by David Llewellyn Davies. But it still lives on in memory. It had a footnote in Edwardian Bradshaw's with its own timetable, that the last train of the day waited for the 2.15pm from Paddington 'on notice being given beforehand'.
Ian Allan Library

Centre right:
Although the Glyn Valley Tramway carried passengers in mixed trains, its main role was transporting road stone from a number of local quarries to Chirk for transfer to the standard gauge.
Ian Allan Library

Below right:
Gobowen was the last stop for southbound expresses before starting an 18-mile dash to Shrewsbury. 'Castle' class No 5073 *Blenheim* on an express of mixed coaching stock, 22 August 1954.
Ian Allan Library/ Brian Morrison

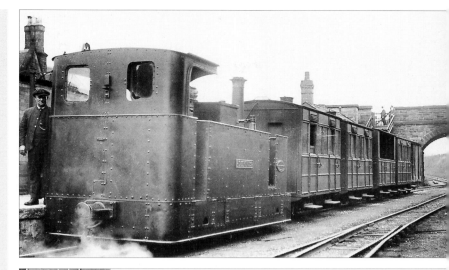

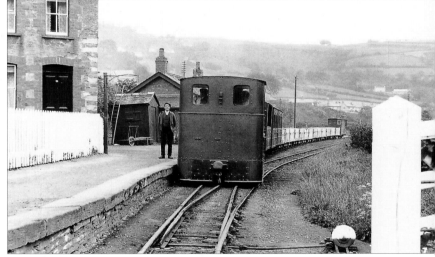

Left:
Wrexham Central in 1904. A Cambrian train for Ellesmere is on the right and an arrival from either Chester or Seacombe is in the bay platform, left. *Ian Allan Library*

Centre left:
Wrexham Central with GWR 0-4-2 tank No 1438 taking water before leaving with the 6.35pm to Ellesmere on 18 August 1962. The branch passenger service was withdrawn three weeks later. *Ian Allan Library*

Below left:
Pannier tank No 1632 shunts south of Hightown on a portion of the Ellesmere branch on 19 September 1963. The branch stayed open for another decade. *Ian Allan Library/M. R. C. Price*

Above right:
The afternoon Chester-Paddington 'Inter-City' leaving Wrexham on 2 September 1964 headed by BR Standard Class 5, No 73026. (Dirty locomotive, clean coaches.) *Ian Allan Library/R. J. Farrell*

Below right:
A Birkenhead-Paddington express between Johnstown and Ruabon, c1965 with BR Standard 4-6-0 No 73006. Johnstown & Hafod station, four miles south of Wrexham, had a sparse passenger service in the years leading to closure in 1960. *Ian Allan Library/A. O. Wynn*

Left:
The Wrexham area was one of the last in which ex-GWR 0-6-2 tanks were in regular use. On 11 September 1965 No 6651 draws a train into the shunting neck to set back into Brymbo branch yard.
Ian Allan Library

Below left:
At Brymbo, trains were shunted into the steelworks over the Vron branch. On 8 May 1965, GWR 2-8-0 No 3813 was handling empty wagons. The steep descent to Wrexham curved sharply left.
G. F. A. Hobbs

Right:
The Wrexham Central-New Brighton service has been cut back in recent years to Bidston with connections to Merseyrail Wirral Line electric services. On 30 August 1965, pannier tank No 4683 was in charge of the 13.06 service to New Brighton. The pannier tanks were successors on this line to the Robinson Great Central Class C13 4-4-2 tanks which worked the service for many years. *G. F. A. Hobbs*

Centre right:
The Croes Newydd branch with gradients of up to 1 in 36 was among the busiest in the Wrexham area for many years and one on which double heading was common. On 30 April 1966 a Stanier '8F' 2-8-0 was being banked on departure from Croes Newydd by 0-6-2 tank No 6697.
Author's collection/M. S. Smith

Below right
Coed Talon was one of three small stations on the busy branch between Brymbo and Mold. Weekday passenger services were withdrawn in March 1950, but a short daily goods continued to run for another 13 years. In April 1959 the branch goods had a second brake van added for Branch Line Society members. The locomotive was 0-6-0 No 44065.
C. A. Appleton

Photographic Souvenir

AND MAP in connection with the

LAST PASSENGER TRAIN

on the

BALA-BLAENAU FESTINIOG BRANCH
of former Great Western Railway

SUNDAY, 22nd JANUARY, 1961

Organised by
THE STEPHENSON LOCOMOTIVE SOCIETY
(Midland Area)

Chronology of the line

1868, 30th May. Festiniog and Blaenau Railway (n.g.—1' 11½") opened from Festiniog—Duffws, 3½ mls., where it met the Festiniog Railway.

1882, 1st November. Bala and Festiniog Railway opened, 22 mls., and worked by the Great Western Railway.

1883, 13th April. Festiniog and Blaenau Railway vested jointly in the B. and F.R. and the G.W.R.

1883, 10th September. Conversion of the F. and B.R. to standard gauge completed, permitting through running from Bala—Blaenau Festiniog.

1910, 1st July. The B. and F.R. and the F. and B.R. acquired by the G.W.R.

1960, 2nd January. Last day of passenger service.

1961, 27th January. Last day of goods service.

The valley between Arenig and Frongoch is scheduled for building of a Liverpool Corporation Reservoir and will involve the flooding of the sites of Capel Celyn and Tyddyn Bridge Halts.

As most of the line runs through mountainous country it is very steeply graded, very largely at 1—50 to 1—75. It rises from Bala to Cwm Prysor, falls to Maentwrog Road and rises again to Manod.

NOTICE No. 53

GREAT WESTERN RAILWAY.

(CHESTER DIVISION).

(For the use of the Company's Servants only).

SIGNAL DEPARTMENT WORK, RUABON SOUTH.

The Signal Department will have occupation at Ruabon South from 7-0 a.m. **Sunday, October 19th,** to 5-0 p.m. on **Friday, October 24th,** or until the work is completed, for the purpose of bringing into use the following new Signals :—

Form	Name.	Position.	Distance from Box.
A	1. Up Main Starting for Middle Box 2. Up Inner Distant	Up side of Main Line	296 yards
B	1. Down Main Inner Home 2. Down Distant for Ruabon Middle 3. Down Main to Goods Running Loop. Inner Home	Down side of Line	8 yards
C	1. Down Main Home (Slotted from Llangollen Line Junction) 2. Down Main to Goods Running Loop Home	Down side of Line	239 yards

Discs will be fixed at the Points leading from Sidings, and at the Points of Crossover Road.

Left:
GWR modernisation at Llangollen Line Junction, Ruabon, in 1924 when, after the takeover of the Cambrian Railways, the GWR was consolidating its presence in Mid Wales. *Author's collection*

Above right:
Ruabon-Barmouth. Dee Valley services shown in the *Birmingham Gazette and Express* pocket timetable of February 1907. *Author's collection*

Centre right:
Until the Dee Valley line was opened Llangollen Road Halt was the railhead from 1852 for a large area of North Wales. The waybill for a wagon shown in 1894, 12 years before it was renamed Whitehurst Halt to avoid confusion with the name Llangollen. Whitehurst closed together with other small stations on the Shrewsbury & Chester main line in 1960. *Author's collection*

Below right:
Black Park Colliery had its own short siding on the main line north of Chirk with a gate across the entrance. In October 1940, soon after the Battle of Britain, it dispatched a wagon load of coal to Barrow for Tarvin, a small station on the Cheshire Lines five miles east of Chester Northgate. *Author's collection*

LLANGOLLEN, BALA, DOLGELLEY, AND BARMOUTH.

(G.W.)	Weekdays						P.M	P.M	P.M	P.M	P.M	P.M	P.M	P.M	P.M	Sundays P.M
	A.M	A.M	A.M	A.M	A.M	A.M										
Birm. (S.H.) dep	P3 55		6 0	8 30		1040	D1248	1050			4 40	5 55	7 013	7 D33		1 D12
W'h'pton (L.L.) „	P4 22		6 43	9 0		1125	1 12	2 15			5 5	6 13	7 57	7 57		5 30
Ruabon .... arr	7 55		9 15	1055	11 20	1 18	2 53	3 45			6 36	8 0	9 7	9 7		5 58
Ruabon ....dep	7 50	8 32	9 40	11 0	12 30	1 40	3 10	3 50	4 10	5 12	6 10	7 8	8 10	9 20	10 45	6 5
Acrefair ...... „	7 54	8 36	9 44	11 5	12 34	1 44	3 14		4 14	5 16	6 14	7 13	8 14	9 24	10 49	6 9
Trevor ...... „	7 58	8 40	9 49	11 8	12 37	1 48	3 18		4 20	5 20	6 18	7 18	8 18	9 28	10 53	6 13
Llangollen „	8 6	8 52	9 58	1120	12 48	2 1	3 28		4 35	5 32	6 30	7 30	8 30	9 46	11 5	6 25
Berwyn .. „	8 12		10 2		12 52	2 5	3 32		4 44		6 35	7 34				6 30
Glyndyfrdwy „	8 19		10 10		1 0	2 10	3 40		4 51		6 44	7 40			11 19	6 39
Carrog ...... „	8 24		10 18		1 5	2 20	3 45		4 57		6 50	7 46				6 45
Corwen.... arr	8 35		10 26		1 10	2 25	3 50	4 20	5 5		6 55	7 53			11 30	6 50
Ruthin .. arr			11 5		1 45		4 35				6 42					
Denbigh .. „			11 21		2 1		4 51				6 58					
Corwen.... dep	8 36		10 30		1 30	2 30	4 0	4 22	5 8		7 55	8 0				
Cynwyd „	8 41		10 35		1 37	2 35	4 6		5 13		8 0	8 5				
Llandrillo .. „	8 46		10 41		1 44	2 41	4 16		5 19		8 5	8 14				
Llanderfel .. „	8 52		10 47		1 55	2 48	4 22		5 25		8 14					
B'la (fm C'r'n) ar	9 10		11 7		2 10	3 5	4 34	4 47	5 42		8 35					
Bala (for Fest'g) d	9 30		11 34						5 44		8 38		9 33			
Festiniog „	10 25		12 25						6 36		9 33					
Bl'nauF'g arr	10 40		12 40						6 50		9 50					
Bala (for Dol'y) d	8 55		10 47			2 50		4 48	5 20		8 14					
Llanuwchllyn „	9 12		11 11			3 10		4 48	5 45		8 37					
Drws-y-Nant „	9 25		11 25						5 51		8 51					
Bont Newydd „	9 35		11 35						6 9		9 1					
Dolgelley.. arr	9 45		11 46						6 20		9 10					
Barmouth „	10 15		12 20						6 56							
Harlech .. „			12 50						7 26							
Portmadoc .. „			1 10						7 53							
Criccieth .. „			1 25						8 5							
Pwllheli .. „			1 55						8 30							
Towyn .. „			12 46						6 30	7 55	S					
Ab'yst'th „			2 20						7 55	9835						

(Several columns carry the vertical note "Motor Car, one cl. only."; one column noted "15 minutes later Sets.")

J Wed. and Sat. only. P Mons. excepted. R Calls to set down. S Sats. only. Y Motor Car, one cl. only. § via Machynlleth, Sats. only.

Footnotes to pages 102 & 103.

C Will not run on Tues., Feb. 12th and 26th. D Dining Car. F Run only on Tues., Feb. 12th and 26th. G 1.25 p.m. Sat. K Mon. & Fri. only. O On Mons. only. Q For Little Hereford. R Fridays only. S Sats. only. T On Mon. and Fris. Hereford dep. 6.30 p.m., and Leominster 6.58 p.m. Y via Dudley. Y Rail Motor Car, one cl. only. † And Broseley.

104

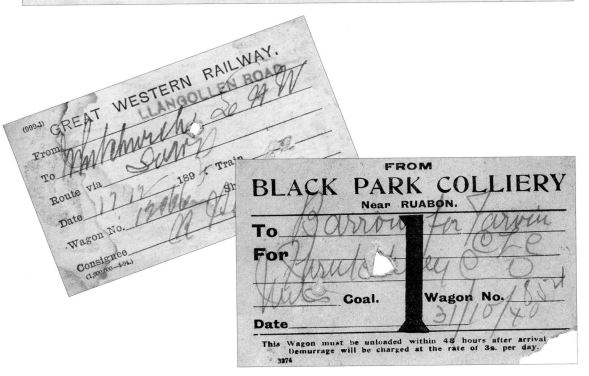

GO BY TRAIN →

EACH WEEKDAY

17th JUNE TO 7th SEPTEMBER 1963

TO

LLANGOLLEN

FROM	TRAIN TIMES		RETURN FARES	
	WEEKDAYS	SATURDAYS ONLY D	First Class	Second Class
	am	am	s d	s d
Liverpool Central Low Level) **A** depart	7-38	8-55	14/3	9/6
Liverpool James Street ...)	7-40	8-57	14/3	9/6
Birkenhead Woodside ... ... ,,	7-50	9-05	13/6	9/—
Rock Ferry ... ... ,,	7-56	9-11	13/3	8/9
Bebington & New Ferry)	7C51	8-34	12/6	8/3
Port Sunlight ... ...) **B**	7C54	8-37	12/6	8/3
Spital ... ... ,,	7C56	8-39	12/—	8/—
Bromborough ... ...)	8C00	8-43	12/—	8/—
Hooton ... ... ,,	8-09	9-23	11/—	7/3
	am	am		
Llangollen ... ... arrive	9-45	11-16		

NOTES : **A**—Change at Rock Ferry in each direction.   **B**—Change at Hooton.
C—Runs 2 minutes later on Saturdays.   **D**—All passengers change at Ruabon.

RETURN ARRANGEMENTS

Passengers return same day from Llangollen by any train having a through connection.

Owing to Passenger Train Alterations during the August Bank Holiday Period, passengers are requested to verify the train services shown hereon as they may be amended.

Children under three years of age, free ; three years and under fourteen, half-fares
(Fractions of a Penny reckoned as a Penny)

TICKETS CAN BE OBTAINED IN ADVANCE AT
STATIONS AND OFFICIAL RAILWAY AGENTS

LONDON
MIDLAND
REGION

Further information will be supplied on application to Stations, Official Railway Agents, or to T. C. BYROM, District Passenger Manager, Lime Street Station, Liverpool (Telephone No. ROYal 9696).

May 1963   J. Wadsworth Ltd., Printers, Grange-over-Sands   BR 35000
F.135/R (Day)

Left:
Llangollen was popular as a day excursion destination for Merseysiders before the Beeching axe. On Saturdays all passengers using two trains from Birkenhead Woodside had to change at Ruabon. *Author's collection*

Below left
A Victorian LNWR single: Euston to Wrexham (WM&CQR) via Crewe, Chester and Hope (Exchange) – a rather roundabout route, especially between Chester and Wrexham. 8 May 1900.

Below right:
A Victorian WM&CQR ticket for an article under 2cwt from Wrexham Central to Upton. Description of article inserted by booking clerk as instructed: bicycle. 7 May 1899.

Right:
Nowhere was the Cambrian Railways presence stronger than at Oswestry where, opposite its headquarters, in the station building, there were the locomotive, carriage and wagon works. In 1957, Collett 0-6-0 No 2239 heads a train of corridor stock on an express – possibly the lunchtime departure from Aberystwyth to Crewe – with a portion detached at Welshpool for Shrewsbury. *Ian Allan Library/J. A. Peden*

London & North Western Ry.
LONDON (EUSTON) (W.) TO
WREXHAM (W.M.& C.Q.)
Via Crewe Chester & Hope (Exchange)
Third]   1(W)(S)   [Class
WREXHAM (WMECQ)
TURN OVER)   FARE 14/11
MY30 061

WM&CQR Ticket for an Article UNDER 2CWTS
Accompanying the Passenger and conveyed at
Mileage Scale at PASSENGER'S RISK
WREXHAM (Central)
To   Upton
On   Ry.
Description of Article
To be inserted by
Booking Clerk.   Bicycle.
CARRIAGE PAID ...s...d
This Ticket must be given up ... SEE BACK

3. Oswestry

The Cambrian is remembered as a Welsh railway company with its headquarters in England, but it is interesting to conjecture how railways in the Welsh borders might have developed had the railway established its headquarters and locomotive, carriage and wagon works at Welshpool in the Severn Valley, 16 miles to the south instead of at Oswestry.

The location was chosen at the first meeting of the directors of the Cambrian after its formation in 1864. The board had before it a petition from the people of Welshpool who claimed that it was more centrally placed than Oswestry, being on the main line to the coast. Welshpool was a substantial station which was built with an upper storey considered large enough for the Cambrian head offices.

However, the directors replied that there had been heavy expenditure at Oswestry in preparation for the development there and a larger station was built with the company headquarters on the first floor. Oswestry grew into one of the busiest small railway towns in Britain, notably because of the railway headquarters and works.

The Cambrian was far from being the first railway to reach Oswestry. Soon after the Shrewsbury & Chester main line was completed, a 2½-mile branch was opened from Gobowen in Christmas week 1848 and it was not until 12 years later that another railway arrived in the town.

The 30-mile Oswestry & Newtown Railway, despite its comparatively short length, took five years to build because of disputes. There was a long drawn out financial argument with the original contractors, which was resolved with the help of the deputy chairman, David Pugh, MP.

In *Bradshaw's Manuals*, he gave his addresses as the Carlton Club, London and Llanerchydol, a village near Welshpool after which one of the first locomotives was named. The chairman of the O&NR was the Earl of Powis, who as owner of Powis Castle, could appoint a director.

Although there were no major engineering works, there were difficulties in acquiring land when a woman landowner and shareholder refused to have the railway near her home, Glansevern, after which another early locomotive was also named.

Eventually the line opened in summer 1860, but its strategic importance as part of a through route to Aberystwyth was reduced only two years later by completion of the Shrewsbury & Welshpool Railway which provided a direct link between London, the West Midlands and the Welsh coast.

Oswestry's third railway – the Oswestry, Ellesmere & Whitchurch – opened on 27 July 1864, two days after the Cambrian Railways Company was formed by the amalgamation of four railway companies. A little-known clause in the Act gave the LNWR running powers over the OE&WR, the Oswestry & Newtown and the Llanidloes & Newtown railways. When the 99-year agreement ended, either party could give four years' notice to terminate it.

For three of the 11 miles between Whitchurch and Ellesmere, the track was laid on brushwood across Whixall Moss, a feature somewhat akin to Chat Moss on the Liverpool & Manchester Railway. The bog had to be conquered, again because a prominent landowner did not want the railway near his property.

An historically interesting local property is a substantial house on Frankton station which has a brick engraved Cambrian Railways coat of arms, suggesting it was the home of a senior official from Oswestry headquarters, which was five miles away. In the Edwardian era, to travel to work, he may have caught the 8.57am and the 5.25pm home, otherwise he faced a two-hour wait.

Close to Oswestry, on the OE&WR, a large Army training camp was established at Park Hall during World War 1, when it was also a German prisoner of war camp. It was served by a halt and a group of goods sidings. The Cambrian carried about a quarter of a million men to and from Park Hall and in his *Story of the Cambrian*, published soon afterwards, C. P. Gasquoine, the respected editor of the *Border*

Left:
Oswestry 1953 – with 0-4-2 tank No 1432 heading a Gobowen motor train. The former GWR station (middle) closed in 1924 when the GWR and Cambrian goods depots were amalgamated. It all closed in 1971.
Ian Allan Library

Above right:
'Barnum' 2-4-0 No 3225 at Oswestry in the late 1930s. The 'Barnums' worked widely on GWR routes in North and Mid Wales including Ruabon-Barmouth. *Ian Allan Library*

Centre right:
Cambrian Railways 4-4-0 No 70 at Llanymynech on an Oswestry-bound stopping train in 1894. Cambrian carriages had double footboards because of low platforms. *R. W. Miller*

Below right:
The three intermediate stations between Llanymynech and Welshpool were often shown as request stops in Cambrian timetables. This is Buttington, looking north with the Cambrian platform, left, and those of the Shrewsbury & Welshpool right. *Jim Peden*

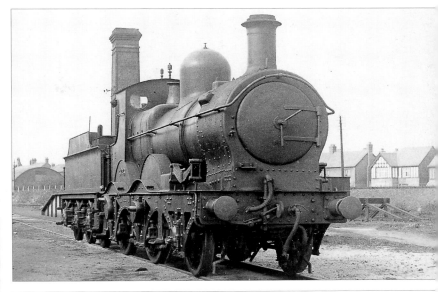

Left:
Passenger services between Whitchurch, Oswestry and Welshpool were withdrawn on 18 January 1965. Hundreds of enthusiasts packed an SLS farewell special. It is seen leaving Oswestry for Whitchurch behind ex-GWR 4-6-0 No 7802 *Bradley Manor*. *R. W. Miller*

Centre left:
A Tanat Valley advertisement. *Author's collection*

Below left:
Ellesmere, junction for the Wrexham branch, was the largest station between Oswestry and Whitchurch. Ivatt Class 2 2-6-0 No 46522 shunts the yard while 0-4-2 tank No 1458 stands on the main line facing Whitchurch having arrived from Oswestry to work the Wrexham branch. *Ian Allan Library/ S. D. Wainwright*

Right:
A Tanat Valley service at Oswestry headed by 2-4-0 tank No 1197. With its sister, No 1196, this was a GWR rebuild of Cambrian locomotives of 1866. They worked the Tanat Valley from the opening of the line in 1904. *Stephenson Locomotive Society*

Counties Advertizer, wrote that the Park Hall traffic placed 'an additional strain on the human and mechanical resources of the company which, however, was most efficiently sustained'.

Of the small network of branches which developed around Oswestry, the most important was that serving the small market town of Llanfyllin, in the hills, 8½ miles west of Llanymynech on the Oswestry & Newtown. The junction lay just north of that with the Potteries, Shrewsbury & North Wales Railway, which approached the main line from the east.

The Llanfyllin branch, dating from 1863, was conventional in contrast to its neighbours. To the north, also serving lightly populated country areas towards the hills, was the Tanat Valley Light Railway, while to the south was another light railway which was narrow gauge, the Welshpool & Llanfair.

Workers from industrial and mining towns who enjoyed a day out in the country, walking and fishing, brought useful traffic to the three intermediate halts on the Llanfyllin branch and because the traffic was unpredictable, local stationmasters were ordered to send staff to them to book passengers. Guards also had

tickets which they had to rubber date stamp before issue. For a branch serving so sparsely populated an area, the timetable was a busy one, with five daily trains each way.

The railways of the Oswestry district were finally completed in Edwardian times by the Tanat Valley Light Railway, authorised in 1899, almost at the close of the Victorian era, and not completed until 1904. Its terminus was at Llangynog, a village much smaller than Llanfyllin and more remote, being several rail miles further from Oswestry. In the mouth of the valley, it was the stem for several short, busy mineral branches, of which the best known were to the quarries at Porthywaen and Nantmawr.

Despite being on the Whitchurch-Aberystwyth main line, Oswestry's busiest passenger line was the 2½-mile GWR branch from Gobowen. Motor trains ('third class only, no heavy luggage') completed the journey in eight minutes and ran seven days a week, although on Sunday mornings they were replaced by Crosville buses.

Passengers for Oswestry were well looked after by the GWR and BR. Just how well, they perhaps never knew because staff instructions

were contained in appendixes which, as was customary, were 'private and not for publication'. They stated that if trains on the Shrewsbury & Chester main line were running late and Oswestry branch trains were despatched without connections, the stationmaster at Gobowen had to arrange to run specials to 'avoid unnecessary delay to through or local passengers'.

Gobowen staff also had to advise if there were any passengers for stations beyond Oswestry in delayed main line trains. But whether specials were run for them south from Oswestry was not stated because that was a matter for a different operating area.

After Nationalisation, the Oswestry District fell within BR's Western Operating Area and stretched towards South Wales, far beyond the old Cambrian Railways system. It encompassed the Manchester & Milford line from Aberystwyth to Carmarthen and extended south from Talyllyn Junction to Pontsticill where its boundary was with the Newport District.

A Victorian verdict on the value of the Cambrian to Oswestry remained true up to closure nearly a century later. In the 1870s, *The Gossiping Guide to Wales* said that while many small towns had been damaged by the introduction of railways, Oswestry had wholly benefited. Its trade had increased, its borders enlarged and shops improved and, added the guide: 'There is a greater air of business about its inhabitants.'

Left:
Blodwell Junction on a summer's day in 1959 with Ivatt Mogul No 46505 running round a ballast train it had worked from Nantmawr Quarries before departing for Oswestry. *Author's collection*

Below left:
Probably the last working to the Nantmawr Quarries – Sulzer Class 24 No 5048 and brake van in which the author travelled on 21 October 1971. The last of the Class 24s were withdrawn in 1980 when B. K. Cooper noted: 'Their passing was mourned'. *R. W. Miller*

Right:
A waybill for wagon No 7915 sent from Oswestry to Whitchurch on 30 November 1894. No note of contents. *Author's collection*

Below right:
Cambrian wagon note of despatch from Bettisfield to Whitchurch on 20 December 1894. Again, there is no note of the nature of the consignment. *Author's collection*

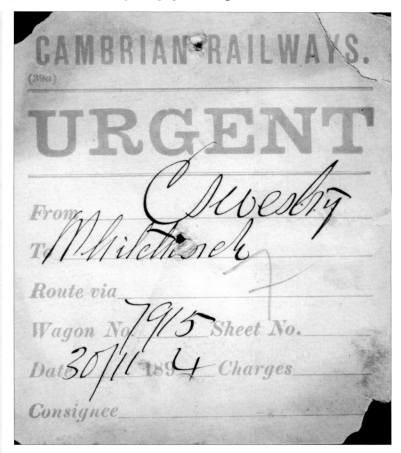

NATIONAL COAL BOARD

SENDER   Date...JAN 1960...194

Sneyd Collieries Limited

COBRIDGE, L.M.S. Rly. (N.S. Section)

A/c   JAMES EDGE LIMITED

TO

LLANRHAIAOR MOCHNANT

G. W. Rly.   C.A.M. ....Secn.

Via CREWE & W'CHURCH

Weight....14....6   T   Cwt.

Owner and No. of Wagon....35154

Description....HOUS COAL GROUP 3.

Consignee....J P JONES   OC

GWR   19 SEP 1947   19__   999-1. O.P.3

From SWANSEA, KINGS DOCK

2A

TO OSWESTRY

___ Rly.___ Secn.

Via

Owner and No. of Wagon 33021

3

Sheets in or on Wagon

Consignee

Contents

50,000 1/46.

GWR   7-1   19__   2829-O.P.1

From AVONMOUTH DOCKS

632899

MARKET GOODS-PERISHABLE

TO OSWESTRY

___ Rly___ Secn.

Via

Owner and No. of Wagon

3

Sheets in or on Wagon

Consignee

Contents Stafford Donning

60,000 BM.938 7/47

Left:
North Staffordshire coal for Mid Wales: a consignment from Sneyd Collieries Ltd at Cobridge to Llanrhaiadr Mochnant, 18 January 1960. The sender is also shown as the National Coal Board. Cobridge is stated – 12 years after Nationalisation – as being on the LMS Railway (NS section) and the destination of the 14-ton load is shown as being on the GWR Cam section. The routeing of the wagon was via Crewe and Whitchurch. *Author's collection*

Below left:
GWR wagon bill for goods to Oswestry from King's Dock, Swansea, is dated shortly before Nationalisation: 19 September 1947. *Author's collection*

Below right:
A perishable market goods consignment from Avonmouth Docks is undated, although the date of the bill print is July 1947. *Author's collection*

Right:
An unidentified Webb 2-2-2-2 of the 'John Hick' class passes the site of Potteries Junction while leaving Shrewsbury with a local train for Stafford. The train is made up of a variety of old coaching stock. *Ian Allan Library*

4. Shrewsbury

The development of Shrewsbury into a junction of five trunk routes and a connecting curve between those to Birmingham and Hereford took almost two decades up to 1867 to complete. It made Shrewsbury the largest railway centre between Chester and Bristol and also the grand junction of the Welsh border.

Shrewsbury featured in several schemes for early railways, which were built not so much to serve it as to join up to form long-distance trunk routes. Their story is told in detail by Richard K. Morriss in *Rail Centres: Shrewsbury*. Briefly, the first to arrive, in 1848-9 were the Shrewsbury & Chester and the Shrewsbury & Birmingham railways – the 'Fighting Shrewsburys' as they were called because of their moves to defeat an LNWR takeover by joining the GWR camp instead. The S&BR was joint with the Shropshire Union Railways (later LNWR), east to Wellington. A 19-mile branch from there to the West Coast main line at Stafford was opened by the LNWR in 1849.

The LNWR/GWR Shrewsbury & Hereford Joint arrived in 1853 after a general shortage of money had held up the start of construction, which did not begin until the end of 1850, some four years after it had been authorised. The contractor was Thomas Brassey, who leased the line, paying a good dividend due to a steady build-up of traffic. In 1858, the company reported six-monthly figures which showed that goods trains had run 96,423 revenue-earning miles and passenger trains, 70,238 miles. This was despite the 1,051yd Dinmore Tunnel still being a single-line bottleneck. (It was not doubled until 1893.)

In 1855, when it was only seven years old, Shrewsbury station was enlarged to meet growing traffic, which was further swollen in 1858 by the arrival of the LNWR with a single-line branch from Crewe. This line was doubled in 1862 as Shrewsbury was linked to Welsh

Left:
Craven Arms with steam railmotor No 74 and a trailer with a second railmotor together forming a three-coach train. Bishop's Castle Railway 0-4-2 tank No 1 – ex-GWR No 567 of 1869 – with original open footplate, shunts on the right. *R. W. Miller*

Below:
Craven Arms and Stokesay – a junction station noted for its large name boards. 2-6-2 tank No 4401 heads a local service. *Stephenson Locomotive Society*

railways advancing towards the Cambrian
coast by the Shrewsbury & Welshpool
LNWR/GWR joint line. It joined the Oswestry
& Newtown near Buttington, where soft
ground defeated plans to tunnel under a low
hill, and the track was therefore laid over the
top of the hill. Local engineers were critical of
the large amount of money wasted on the
aborted tunnel scheme.

Hanwood, a village five miles from
Shrewsbury, became a notable, if little known,
centre of railway interest. It was the junction of
a five-mile single-track branch, also jointly
operated, which ran from the S&WR at
Cruckmeole (or Hanwood) Junction to Minsterley.
Far better remembered is the narrow gauge
Snailbeach District Railways – a mineral line of
some three miles which ran from Minsterley to
the neighbouring village of Pontesbury where it
interchanged traffic with the standard gauge.

Only days after the S&WR opened in winter
1862, the Severn Valley Railway was completed
between Shrewsbury and Hartlebury near
Worcester, a branch which has been featured in
an earlier title in the *A View from the Past*
series.

Finally, Shrewsbury's main network was
completed in 1867 by the Abbey Foregate curve,
another LNWR/GWR joint line which linked
the Birmingham and Hereford routes and
created a Shrewsbury-avoiding direct link
between the West Midlands and the Cambrian
coast via Welshpool.

Another Welsh link of which Shrewsbury
became the focus was the Central Wales line,
constructed progressively in the 1860s
southwest from Craven Arms (& Stokesay until
1974) to Swansea. The 96 miles of complicated
ownership were predominantly those of the
LNWR, which fought the GWR for traffic from
South Wales to northern England and beyond.
The extra traffic it added to the S&HR over
the 20 miles between Shrewsbury and Craven
Arms was always well within the capacity of
the section. Just before Knucklas, the first
station in Wales beyond Shropshire, the single
line crosses a 13-arch viaduct, which is among
the most striking engineering features of the line.

In 1898, half a century after Shrewsbury joint station opened, a respected guide book author said it reminded him of the primitive days of railroad travelling. Its image was soon to change, however, because early in the Edwardian era it was rebuilt for a second time and became the attractive station we know today. A street-level entrance hall was dug out below the level of the platforms, which were extended over the River Severn.

The two main platforms were lengthened to over 1,200ft so that each could handle two trains at once. The station was controlled by seven signalboxes, of which the largest, which still dominates the south end, had nearly 200 levers. In Edwardian days, the station staff totalled about 160.

Staff handled Shrewsbury's three express services: Paddington-Birkenhead, North to West, and to the coast by the 'Cambrian Coast Express' which was so named in 1922. This was 12 years after through services had been introduced following the opening of the GWR direct route between Paddington and Birmingham Snow Hill. In later years, the

Birkenhead expresses were heavily promoted by the GWR, having the distinction of being the subject of the company's second *Through the Window* route book. It noted of Shrewsbury: 'The enormous number of rails here impresses every traveller.'

The Birkenhead route was Shrewsbury's only main line express service until the Severn Tunnel opened in 1886 and the GWR introduced a North to West express route. It was an immediate success because long-distance passengers no longer had to change trains with the Midland Railway at

Below:
'Happy days', wrote retired railway officer Nigel Payton as a caption to this commercial postcard of an LMS streamliner passing Crewe Gresty Lane No 1 box. The unidentified Stanier Pacific is heading a long, head-boarded express of GWR corridor stock from the West of England. The clean condition of the locomotive suggests it was returning from Shrewsbury on a running-in turn from Crewe Works. *Author's collection*

Right:
The LNWR Severn Bridge Junction signalbox dates from the rebuilding and resignalling of the station at the turn of the 20th century. Today, it is the biggest manual signalbox in Britain. From the top windows the staff can shout across the layout to engineers working on platform signals.
Author's collection

Below:
LMS 'Princess Royal' class Pacific No 6202, nicknamed 'Turbomotive', seen at Shrewsbury in the late 1930s. It was built by Stanier in 1935 to assess the uses of turbine locomotive power.
Ian Allan Library

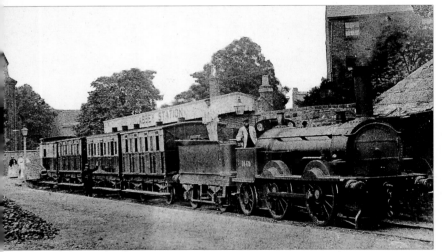

Left:
A West of England express climbs away from Shrewsbury towards Crewe on a summer's evening, 30 July 1952. 'Royal Scot' No 46114 *Coldstream Guardsman* was working through from Pontypool Road. *Ian Allan Library/L. N. Owen*

Centre left:
In contrast to the glory of General station, Shrewsbury Abbey station was primitive. In the early 1870s, soon after it was opened, a passenger train of the Potteries, Shrewsbury & North Wales Railway awaits departure. It is headed by ex-LNWR 0-4-2 No 1859 with open footplate and four-wheeled tender. The coaches are also four-wheeled. *Ian Allan Library*

Below left:
Shropshire and Montgomeryshire Railway locomotive No 6 *Thisbe* on the 3.30pm mixed Shrewsbury to Llanymynech leaving Shrewsbury West on 6 April 1926. *LCGB/K. Nunn collection*

Right:
Unrebuilt 'Patriot' No 45538 *Giggleswick* in green livery, with the 7.5am Plymouth-Liverpool express departing from Shrewsbury 21 minutes late on Sunday, 27 April 1952. *Ian Allan Library/E. D. Bruton*

Birmingham New Street and Bristol.
Shrewsbury was the mid-point of the longest
through journey, the Aberdeen-Penzance via
Crewe, which southbound took 11 hours to
Shrewsbury and another 10 to Cornwall.

Services, joint with the LNWR, developed
progressively. Ten years after the tunnel
opened, an Anglo-Scottish service was
introduced to and from Bristol and South
Wales. Expresses departed Bristol and Cardiff at
9.30am and reached Glasgow Central at 8pm.
They ran nonstop through the 15 intermediate
stations between Shrewsbury and Hereford.

Local passenger traffic was light, an
Edwardian *Baedeker Guide* describing the three
intermediate stations between Shrewsbury and
Church Stretton as 'unimportant', but in later
years Dorrington became more important with
a daily London milk train running to a depot
close to Marylebone station. Several local
stations were well used but others on the North
to West between Crewe and Shrewsbury never
developed beyond being request stops.

One of the complications of S&HR operations
occurred when locomotives were running light,
returning from Chester and intermediate places
to Pontypool Road. If they did not need to call

at Hereford shed for coal and water, drivers
gave two short whistles to the signalman at
Moreton-on-Lugg, the last station, 4½ miles
north. The signalman then advised his
colleague at Barr's Court Junction who had to
find out from the joint inspector whether the
locomotive was to be routed through Barr's
Court or Barton stations.

The Shrewsbury & Welshpool joint line
carried two local services, the longest stretching
49 miles from Stafford in the east to Welshpool.
Some trains ran only part way and served three
small stations between Wellington and
Shrewsbury. The second service was to
Minsterley.

Hanwood was of particular interest as it was
an interchange point for goods traffic with the
Shropshire & Montgomeryshire Light Railway,
which had its headquarters at a minor
passenger terminal in Shrewsbury called Abbey.
On the opposite side of the London-Holyhead
road was the historic church.

The S&MLR ran for 18 miles through almost
empty countryside to meet the Cambrian
Railways at Llanymynech. It closed to regular
passenger services in 1933, although
interchange of goods, mineral and cattle traffic

continued at Hanwood under conditions laid down in sectional appendices of the S&H Joint. Several years after the demise of the S&MLR passenger service, Bradshaw's still carried a footnote in the Minsterley table stating that Abbey station at Shrewsbury was about half a mile from General. This was prophetic for during World War 2, the station handled troop specials for men stationed at various ammunition depots served by the line. Troops going on leave might have noticed that they needed time to walk the half a mile between stations.

Hereford

Hereford grew to be one of the most important junctions of the Marches, from the opening of the Shrewsbury & Hereford Railway late in December 1853. This was followed at the beginning of January 1854 by the arrival from the south of the Newport, Abergavenny & Hereford Railway, which established Barton as Hereford's station on a through route between Shrewsbury and Newport. In 1855, the broad gauge Hereford, Ross & Gloucester Railway reached Barr's Court, a station more centrally situated. Major growth came in the 1860s with

completion of the Worcester & Hereford Railway in 1861 and the opening of a short line connecting the NA&HR with the tip of the HR&GR in 1866 to allow through expresses to be switched from Barton station to Barr's Court.

An Edwardian guide book stressed the convenience of Barr's Court, from which 'any part of the kingdom can be reached as no fewer than five lines run into it. The Shrewsbury & Hereford is the direct route to the north. The Hereford, Ross & Gloucester line, with a branch from Ross to Monmouth and Chepstow, thence via the Severn Tunnel, Bristol and Bath, connects with London. The Newport, Abergavenny & Hereford line, with a branch from Hereford to Worcester, connects with the Midland counties and London. The Hereford, Hay & Brecon line, worked by the Midland company, connects with the most important parts of Wales.'

Below:
The most distinctive of S&MR locomotives, *Gazelle* was an 0-4-2 well tank built by Dodman in 1893. The coach is a former London County Council horse tram body. *LGRP/Bucknall collection*

Above:
Shrewsbury was a busy cross-roads for goods traffic. GWR Class 2800 No 3830 crosses Crewe Junction as it leaves the Chester line on 12 June 1964 with a southbound goods made up of four-wheeled wagons. An impressive array of signals controlled the junction. *Ian Allan Library/Derek Cross*

Right:
'Castle' class No 5061 *Earl of Birkenhead* awaits departure from Shrewsbury with a weekday-only Margate-Birkenhead in 1959. The train carried a buffet car for the entire journey and through coaches from Sandwich, Deal, Dover and Folkestone to Birkenhead and through coaches from Hastings, Eastbourne and Brighton to Chester. *Ian Allan Library/ S. D. Wainwright*

Left:
The Shrewsbury & Hereford main line was punctuated by a string of rural halts with small wooden shelters and prominent nameboards. On 10 June 1957, a three-coach local heads north nonstop through All Stretton Halt, 11 miles south of Shrewsbury. It was served by only two weekday services. After opening in 1936 it was closed temporarily 1943-6 and finally in 1958. *Ian Allan Library/ Michael Mensing*

Below:
No 6000 *King George V* on a Wirral Railway Circle special passing the site of Marshbrook station, five miles north of Craven Arms on 5 October 1974. *R. W. Miller*

Of Shrewsbury's two express routes – Paddington to Birkenhead and North to West of England via the Severn Tunnel – that to Merseyside was the more unusual, for expresses changed their character midway with long-distance nonstop runs to Birmingham giving way to rather slower semi-fast services serving towns only short distances apart.

In spring 1910, the 2.15pm 'Birmingham and North Express' from Paddington slipped coaches at Banbury and Leamington and reached Birmingham Snow Hill nonstop in 2hr 20min. After a five-minute stop, it continued to Wolverhampton (another five-minute stop) and after slipping a third coach at Wellington, reached Shrewsbury at 5.45pm. After detaching

a tea car, it continued to Gobowen (with Oswestry connections), Chirk (conditional), Wrexham, Rossett (conditional) and Chester (General), where after reversal, often in the north-end bay platforms, it continued nonstop to Rock Ferry, leaving passengers for the West Kirby branch to catch a following local service. Arrival at Birkenhead Woodside was at 7.46pm and at Liverpool Landing Stage at 8pm. Against the 110 miles to Birmingham covered in 140 minutes, the 100 miles to Birkenhead took 191 minutes.

The pattern and frequency of the Paddington-Birkenhead expresses changed little through the years. The nearest they came to being named was in the 1960s when the Western Region called a weekday restaurant car service between London and Shrewsbury 'The Inter-City'. Again, it was fast to Birmingham Snow Hill and then slower northwards. It terminated at Chester, which meant that it was not considered to be a London-Merseyside service complementary or alternative to Liverpool Lime Street-Euston. Gone was all such pretence

as cherished by the GWR half a century before.

A feature of down West of England express workings was the need to keep time because of connections at Crewe with Scottish services, which could only be held for a few minutes because of pathing difficulties further north. Retired staff who worked on the down side at Crewe still remember the nightmare of the early 1960s when they had to placate passengers arriving on late-running West of England services who found they had to wait for up to six hours to go north.

North to West services were booked nonstop between Shrewsbury and Hereford, allowing about 70 minutes for the 50 miles. Some through expresses to and from Manchester London Road and Liverpool Lime Street to Plymouth carried through coaches for Torquay. Manchester-Cardiff expresses included through coaches from Birkenhead forward from Shrewsbury.

With Shrewsbury being a town surrounded by villages, there were never any intensive local services. On the Shrewsbury & Hereford, seven weekday trains were slotted in between through expresses and goods trains, but not all

called at intermediate stations, several of which by winter 1950 were no more than passenger request stops. On Sundays, the service was reduced to two afternoon services which called only at Craven Arms & Stokesay, Ludlow, Woofferton and Leominster.

The sparsity of local services on main lines could be associated with the withdrawal of Sunday services on connecting lines. Hereford was without Sunday trains on the Hereford, Ross & Gloucester line, a useful weekday feeder as well as being a purely local service of eight trains each way, and on the Hereford, Hay & Brecon, which for many years carried four trains each way on weekdays.

Branch line timetables often reflected a rural way of life, sometimes with a service from country to town in early afternoon and a return towards midnight on Friday before the line closed for the weekend.

Local services over the Chester & Shrewsbury were included in the main line timetable. They were sparse, with gaps of up to five hours at stations and halts along the thinly populated 17 miles between Shrewsbury and Gobowen.

Left:
Marshbrook was a typical wayside station on the Shrewsbury & Hereford Railway. It was used by several weekday stopping trains which took 40min from Shrewsbury, 15 miles to the north. *Stephenson Locomotive Society/W. A. Camwell*

Above right:
A Saturday special: 4-6-0 No 1025 *County of Radnor* approaches Leominster with a formation of mixed coaches on 18 June 1960. The express is running under clear lower quadrant signals. *T. Radway*

Centre right:
Leominster signalbox dominated the station. 0-4-2 tank No 1455 is returning to shed after yard and station pilot duties, 18 June 1960. The platform used by Bromyard and Worcester branch trains is far left. *T. Radway*

Below right:
Enthusiasts sometimes caught Minsterley branch trains to visit the narrow gauge Snailbeach District Railways which ran from Pontesbury to several mines in the neighbouring hills. The scene is Snailbeach locomotive shed, which still stands.
Ian Allan Library

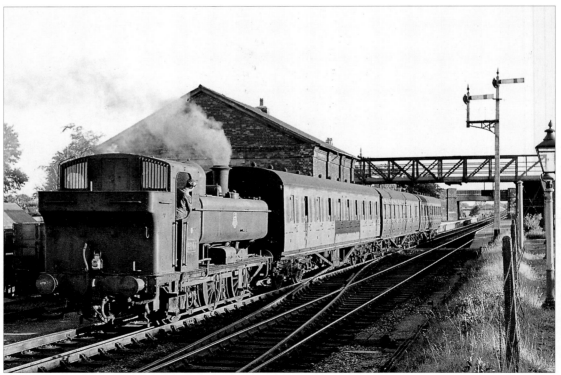

Above left:
No 5030 *Shirburn Castle* passes Onibury on the 8.45am West to North express from Plymouth in 1951. Before closure in 1958, Onibury was a little-used station and was only a request stop for some S&H local services. *Ian Allan Library/C. R. L. Coles*

Below left:
Woofferton, junction for Bewdley, with pannier tank No 4641 shunting empty stock which will form the 7.50pm to Birmingham Snow Hill, 10 June 1957. *Ian Allan Library/ Michael Mensing*

Above right:
The acceleration of LNWR Euston-Shrewsbury services in summer 1905 reduced journey times to just over three hours, making them several minutes quicker than the GWR Paddington-Shrewsbury services of about the same period. *Author's collection*

Below right:
The Wirral Railway Circle ran some 60 railtours 1969-73. The 'Royal Giants' of May 1973 was among the most memorable. *Author's collection*

LONDON AND NORTH WESTERN RAILWAY.

Greatly improved and accelerated Services between

EUSTON
AND
LEAMINGTON, BIRMINGHAM, WOLVERHAMPTON, SHREWSBURY.

1 hr. 50 mins.   2 hours.   2 hrs. 30 mins.   3 hrs. 10 mins.

MAY AND JUNE, 1905.—WEEK DAYS.

Euston Station, London, *April*, 1905.

BREAKFAST, LUNCHEON, or DINING CARS on all the principal Trains.

FREDERICK HARRISON, *General Manager*.

WIRRAL RAILWAY CIRCLE
"NOTHING SATISFIES BUT THE BEST"

President: Rev. S. J. Wright, B.A.

5th ANNIVERSARY - OCTOBER, 1973

The "ROYAL GIANTS" Rail Tour at Hereford, showing 92203 "BLACK PRINCE" and 6000 "KING GEORGE V".

The Wirral Railway Circle proudly presents its 163rd Fixture the "Summers Ore", Industrial Rail Tour of B.S.C. Shotton (WRC Industrial Rail Tour No. 21) and Fixture 164 Bala Lake Railway Tour (WRC Special Train on Preserved Lines No. 10) to commemorate the Fifth Anniversary of the Formation of the Society in October, 1968.

(The Summers Ore is the 85th Special Train to be run by WRC.)

Founder Members: Chris Magner, Richard Thomson, Steve Senior, Paul Boot, Rev. S. J. Wright.

Present Council: Rev. S. J. Wright (President), Christopher Bakalarski (Treasurer), Alec Rodgers (Secretary), Chris Magner (Publicity Officer and Journal Editor), Richard Thomson (Tours Officer), John Allcock (Membership Secretary), Brian Fiddler and John Ryan.

Rail Tours Division: Chris Magner, Chris Bakalarski, Richard Thomson (Rail Tour Organisers) Paul Balmer, John Allcock, John Belk, Ian Jamieson (Booking Officers). Steve Senior (Headboards Officer).

𝕻𝖍𝖔𝖙𝖔𝖌𝖗𝖆𝖕𝖍𝖎𝖈 𝕾𝖔𝖚𝖛𝖊𝖓𝖎𝖗

in connection with the

LAST TRAIN

on the

SHROPSHIRE and MONTGOMERYSHIRE RAILWAY

SUNDAY, 20th MARCH, 1960

Organised by

THE STEPHENSON LOCOMOTIVE SOCIETY

(Midland Area)

Chronology of the line

Potteries, Shrewsbury and North Wales Railway o. 13th August, 1866, cl. 21st December, 1866, re-opened December, 1868, closed and abandoned as from 22nd June, 1880.

Re-opened as Shropshire and Montgomeryshire Railway on 13th Apl. 1911, (Criggion branch on 21st February, 1912).

Passenger services ceased from 6th November, 1933.

Government control assumed as from September, 1939.

1941—main line (Shrewsbury-Llanymynech) requisitioned by WD.

1947—WD Military status to WD Civilian status.

1948—become part of B.R.—the Railway Executive, Western Region. (Only the Criggion branch was affected by this).

1959—Military depots closed and tracks lifted. Criggion branch closed completely after cessation of quarry traffic in December.

1960—29th February, civilian rail traffic facilities ceased; the last train actually worked from Abbey station, Shrewsbury, on 26th February, when work commenced upon a connection from Abbey goods yard to the Severn Valley branch of the W.R. From this date the outlet for military traffic became Llanymynech.

As soon as all W.D. equipment has been removed the line will be formally handed back to B.R. (W.R.)—dismantling will follow.

153

Left:
W. A. Camwell's funereal souvenirs are now collectors' items. The Shropshire & Montgomeryshire 'obit' acknowledges the help of the historian Eric S. Tonks.
Author's collection

Below left:
Shrewsbury platform ticket dated 10 June 1957 still carrying the title GW & LNWR Joint.

Below right:
Shropshire & Montgomeryshire Railway third class single. Destination station is printed Shrewsbury S&M, rather than Abbey station.

Right:
Presthope, one of nine stations and halts between Much Wenlock and Craven Arms, closed to passengers at the end of 1951, but goods traffic continued for another 12 years from the Buildwas end.
Stephenson Locomotive Society/ W. A. Camwell

5. Shrewsbury & Hereford: Branches

As well as being a long section of a north-to-south through route, the Shrewsbury & Hereford line also became the trunk for a fascinating collection of branches which proliferated over 40 years. All were full of variety, charm, character and individuality. Some were long: the Severn Valley route stretched for 40 miles from Shrewsbury to Hartlebury; the Hereford, Hay & Brecon for nearly 30 miles; and there was the Kington cluster with Titley, one of Britain's smallest country junctions, at its heart, a place where you could catch a train travelling north, south, east and west.

All these branches had passenger and goods traffic for many years and were Great Western with the exception of Woofferton-Tenbury, which was LNWR/GW Joint, and the HH&B,

very much a Midland outpost. Most northerly of the S&H branches was the Severn Valley. Although beginning at Shrewsbury's railway heart, the first 11½ miles, from Burnt Mill Junction to Buildwas, were supervised by the GWR Divisional Superintendent at Chester.

Craven Arms

Craven Arms, 20 miles south of Shrewsbury, grew into the junction of three lines of differing character and importance, each owned by a separate company. The only common factors were that they were standard gauge and single line. They joined the S&H main line but there were no timed passenger connections or exchange of traffic, or through running.

The Central Wales Railway, now downgraded,

Left:
Plowden, one of four intermediate stations on the Bishop's Castle Railway, which found a niche in Victorian Bradshaw's. The railway's timetable showed four daily passenger trains between Bishop's Castle and Craven Arms & Stokesay. Shrewsbury & Hereford local services and those to Bishop's Castle were separated by 160 pages, but connections of varying lengths could be worked out from them.
J. A. Peden

Above:
The Bishop's Castle Railway remains among the most fascinating of Britain's small, forgotten railways. The scene, probably in late Victorian years, shows a mixed train about to leave Craven Arms. *LGRP/R. W. Miller*

Left:
Longville, one of 11 stations on the Wellington-Craven Arms line lost its passenger and goods services at the same time as Presthope.
The photograph shows 2-6-2 tank No 4401 on the 3.10pm Wellington-Craven Arms on 21 April 1951. *Stephenson Locomotive Society/W. A. Camwell*

was by far the longest and busiest. The name Craven Arms was derived from a fortified manor house, which is a landmark of the Marches route. It never became a traffic bottleneck, partly because there were no stations or halts on the main line between the station and branch junctions.

The Craven Arms-Much Wenlock Railway branched from the S&H at Marsh Farm Junction, some three miles north of the main line station and formed part of a through route via Buildwas to Wellington, where it met the Shrewsbury & Birmingham Railway. Much Wenlock station lay at the top of a steep climb from the River Severn and is held in memory by a Don Breckon painting.

The branch was constructed southwest from Much Wenlock, the first terminus being Presthope, reached in 1864. Completion followed three years later after delays because of the need for a deviation, including a short tunnel, to meet landowners' objections.

The course of the trackbed under Wenlock Edge is easily followed and Shropshire rail journeys, possibly made by the poet A. E. Housman, who immortalised the Edge, are considered by Robin Shaw in *Housman's Places* published by the Housman Society.

Bishop's Castle Railway

The third of the Craven Arms branches was the Bishop's Castle Railway which, like the infant Shropshire & Montgomeryshire, was eccentric. But there the comparison ended, for while the S&MLR became valuable during World War 2 serving the large ammunition dumps and soldiers manning them, the BCR never grew up and closed for ever on 20 April 1935 while the war clouds were still gathering.

The BCR's existence was precarious from birth and it never succeeded in its territorial ambition to be a link of almost 20 miles between the Oswestry & Newtown Railway near Newtown, and the S&HR just north of Craven Arms. Incorporated in 1861, it included a 2¼-mile branch to the small and ancient borough of Bishop's Castle from Lydham Heath, where a reversal was necessary and

time-consuming, although perhaps this was not considered too much of a handicap because of the slow pace of country life there.

Passenger and goods services finally began in 1866 but within a year the line closed. *Bradshaw's Manual* for 1869 stated that the rolling stock was seized by judgement creditors and traffic was being conducted by a receiver, adding that 'no accounts of receipts or working expenses appear to be issued'.

It reopened in 1877 and a service of four daily trains each way was detailed, including one Parliamentary, with Shrewsbury connections, in Bradshaw's timetable. It received the same typographical prominence as services on the Central Wales Railway, set out on an opposite page, and of those between Shrewsbury and Stafford, whose ownership was stated to be the Shropshire Union-LNWR. When it finally closed, T. R. Perkins wrote in *The Railway Magazine*: 'Although many people who were well acquainted with the line were aware that it could not possibly carry on much longer, the closing must have caused regret to a large number of railwayists.'

Right:
An Edwardian Bishop's Castle Railway timetable shows trains 'in connection with' the Shrewsbury & Hereford main line. There is still local affection for the railway's memory. Time Lines, the Bishop's Castle Railway and Transport Museum, was badly damaged by fire in November 2000. Full restoration began soon afterwards.
Ian Allan Library

Left:
Horderley, one of four intermediate stations between Craven Arms and Bishop's Castle. It was closest to the junction of the Shrewsbury & Hereford main line. *LGRP/Ian Allan Library*

Below:
A nostalgic scene at Plowden in the Edwardian era sees locomotive No 1 with ex-LNWR chain brake coaches.
LGRP/Ian Allan Library

Above:
On the last day of passenger services between Woofferton and Tenbury Wells, 29 July 1961, ex-GWR tank No 1445 waits at Woofferton with an auto train. *Stephenson Locomotive Society*

Left:
After the withdrawal of the Woofferton service, Tenbury Wells retained a passenger link to Bewdley and Kidderminster for another year. *Stephenson Locomotive Society*

Above:
Neen Sollars was one of the isolated stations
between Tenbury and Bewdley.
Stephenson Locomotive Society/W. A. Camwell

Woofferton-Tenbury-Bewdley

Victorian travellers were sometimes the victim
of railway companies who were reluctant to
publicise how far some stations were from the
towns and villages they purported to serve. A
classic case was Cleobury Mortimer where
some two miles of twisting roads separated
town and station, yet neither GWR timetables
nor Bradshaw's warned passengers of this fact.

However, not all those arriving or departing
from the town had to make the road journey.
The lucky ones were those making connections
with trains on the Cleobury Mortimer & Ditton
Priors Light Railway, which ran for 12 miles
through the almost empty countryside and, like
the Shropshire & Montgomeryshire, served
remote wartime ammunition depots. It
stemmed from a single line through Wyre

Forest from Bewdley to the S&H at Woofferton,
where the station name was spelt in several
different ways. It was predominantly Great
Western, as the company wholly owned the
15½ miles between Bewdley and Tenbury, and
jointly owned the remaining 5½ miles west to
Woofferton with the LNWR.

Construction progressed eastwards in the
mid-Victorian years. Tenbury was reached in
1861, with the assistance of the S&H, which
disposed of part of the Leominster Canal, and it
was completed with a connection to the Severn
Valley Railway in 1864. The River Severn was
crossed close to the approach to the junction at
Bewdley by the short but distinctive Dowles
Viaduct. Today, the pillars of this viaduct can be
seen from the carriage window of trains on
today's Severn Valley Railway, and from the
riverside at Bewdley.

The Kington Branches

Just over six miles south of Woofferton, the
small market town of Leominster became the
hub of branches running east and west from the
main line. Locally based Victorian promoters
hoped for a line from Worcester to the

73

Cambrian coast, but after their hopes were dashed, they set about opening up the remote countryside stretching west from Leominster to the Welsh border.

The 13½-mile single-track Leominster & Kington Railway was incorporated in 1854 and opened three years later. It was leased to Brassey & Field under arrangements which provided shareholders with 4% dividends as traffic steadily increased. The lease passed to the GWR & West Midland Railway in 1862. After the branch opened, Kington became a railhead for much of West Wales with daily coaches to Aberystwyth, then becoming popular with ever-growing numbers of Victorian tourists.

The Kington branch gained a fresh increase traffic in 1875 with the completion of a six-mile branch from Titley, where a station was built some distance from the village, to Presteign, the county town of Radnor. This was a year after Titley had a second branch, built by other promoters, from Eardisley on the Hereford, Hay & Brecon Railway. It opened a few days before the Leominster & Kington Railway was extended six miles west to New Radnor, the centre of expanding, well-established quarries.

Worcester-Bromyard-Leominster

Like the Woofferton-Bewdley branch a few miles to the north, the 24-mile route between Worcester and Leominster had a short but complicated history. It took 36 years to complete and was open as a through route for only 55 years. Promoters were faced with a shortage of money, difficulties in acquiring land and conquering a quite hilly terrain – it climbed to a summit of 685ft above sea level near Fencote. The Worcester, Bromyard & Leominster Railway was incorporated in 1861, chaired by Sir Charles Hastings, founder of the British Medical Association, but only eight years later, the promoters abandoned the

Below:
An SLS railtour marked the centenary of the Leominster-Kington branch in July 1957 with GWR 0-4-2T No 1455. Such were the complexities of railway building in the Marches that the tour notes referred to eight companies concerned with the building of 70 miles of main line and the branches which the tour covered. This was probably the only occasion on which the Kington platform was ever described as crowded.
Author's collection

Above:
Cleobury Mortimer 1938.
A pannier tank heads a
Kidderminster-Woofferton late
afternoon service. Two of the
three coaches are GWR
clerestory stock. Tall water
tanks dominate both platform
ends. On the right, a Ditton
Priors train awaits departure.
Stephenson Locomotive Society

Right:
Pembridge had a substantial
station building but
comparatively few passengers.
The Leominster-Kington
branch carried only weekday
passenger services.
*Stephenson Locomotive Society/
W. A. Camwell*

Left:
A busy autumn 1947 evening at Titley with 0-4-2 tank No 3574 with a Leominster-New Radnor train and a Presteign branch local headed by pannier tank No 7420.
Stephenson Locomotive Society

Below:
Eardisley on the Midland branch from Hereford to Three Cocks was a junction with the Great Western branch which ran south from Titley.
Stephenson Locomotive Society

proposed 12-mile section from Leominster to Bromyard, which, although small, was the only town of any size that the railway could serve. A short time later, the GWR agreed to work the line from Bromyard to Worcester, and it opened in two sections between 1874 and 1877.

Meanwhile the abandoned section had been revived and the Leominster & Bromyard Railway was formed in 1874. A decade later, it was completed as far as Steens Bridge, which remained the terminus for 13 years until the line was extended to Bromyard in 1897, under GWR auspices.

The branch stemmed from the Worcester & Hereford at Bransford Road Junction and its trains used both stations at Worcester, calling at Foregate Street and terminating at Shrub Hill. Serving lightly populated areas, it had a weekday-only service, but this was slightly more intensive than on many other lines which were almost totally rural, five trains each way calling at five intermediate stations.

Passenger traffic slowly ebbed away and Leominster to Bromyard was closed completely in August 1952, while Worcester to Bromyard remained open for another 12 years. Western Region timetables carried footnotes warning passengers that some late afternoon and evening trains were third class only with limited accommodation. Were either notes needed? Did the trains, often auto formations, ever carry any first class passengers, and were they ever crowded?

Below:
Clee Hill stone transhipment terminal with narrow gauge rails flanking both sides of a well of standard gauge tracks. The shunter is an LNWR open-cab saddle tank. *R. W. Miller*

Ludlow & Clee Hill Railway

The only mineral branch off the Shrewsbury & Hereford was by far the most spectacular: the 6-mile line from Ludlow which included a 1¼-mile rope-worked incline that lifted wagons 600ft up the hillside on a gradient of 1 in 12. It was connected to a mile-long summit 1,250ft above sea level, which was locomotive-worked to granite quarries. Bitterley yard at the incline foot was troublesome to operate, too, being approached on a gradient of 1 in 20. The L&CHR was opened privately in 1864 and three years later, the owners signed a working agreement with the GWR and LNWR and the line was absorbed jointly by them from January 1893. Traffic built up continually and in the 1920s it was totalling some 6,000 tons a week.

The incline was closed two years before complete closure of the branch in late 1962.

One perk for men working the branch was officially recognised in the S&H Sectional Appendix under the heading 'Trolleying of Platelayers from Bitterley to Ludlow in the evenings'. It stated: 'When the working of the branch will admit, the undermen going home to Ludlow in the evenings may make use of the trolley.' The trolley was to be signalled as a train, the speed restricted to a maximum of 10mph and the signalman at Clee Hill Junction advised of its arrival by the man in charge.

Hereford, Hay & Brecon

In a 36-page Branch Line Society itinerary for a Manchester Piccadilly-Hereford railtour of

15 July 1958, Dr M. Dean noted that the Hereford, Hay & Brecon was the only company to build *from* Hereford.

The Midland's arrival added a useful dimension to the routes and liveries of Hereford's railways through its development of the Hereford, Hay & Brecon which formed about a quarter of the Midland route to South Wales from its own territory at Worcester. It provided 28 miles of the 108 miles between Worcester and Swansea via Malvern, Hereford and Brecon, although the latter town could be bypassed by goods trains, reducing the overall distance by nearly nine miles. It was a through route which crossed the Marches from east to west rather than one which served them. The HH&BR, incorporated in summer 1859, was to run from Hereford Barr's Court to Brecon, but the 34-mile route was truncated to Three Cocks Junction (almost 27 miles) and the 7½ miles west to Talyllyn Junction was transferred to the Mid-Wales Railway, soon to become part of the Cambrian. The 4¼ miles from Talyllyn to Brecon became the tip of the Brecon & Merthyr Railway.

The HH&BR bought the Hay Railway and adapted three miles of the tramway as it advanced west up the Wye Valley between 1862 and 1864. It was worked by the contractor,

Thomas Savin, who was much involved with Welsh railways. The HH&BR suffered a further setback to its aspirations when its amalgamation with the Brecon & Merthyr was ruled illegal. The Midland, which had started running goods trains to Hereford from Worcester in 1868 leased the HH&BR, a move which led to absorption in 1876.

In the interim there had been a classic locomotive and wagon blockade by the GWR at Hereford, which resulted in the Midland having to use a temporary terminus at Hereford, called Moorfields, for five years. In 1893, Midland trains reached Barr's Court over a short link to Barton & Brecon Curve Junction, opened by the S&H Joint.

The Midland never ran expresses to South Wales, partly because the HH&B was heavily used by goods including a service which the LNWR developed between South Wales and Birmingham. Local trains calling at the 10 intermediate stations between Hereford and Brecon, took about 1hr 30min, while passengers making a through journey on one or two weekday trains to Swansea St Thomas faced journeys of about four hours, including a wait of 10 or more minutes at Brecon Joint station, one of more than 20 intermediate stops.

Left:
Sentinel 0-4-0 No 68164 approaching Clee Hill incline top with stone from the quarries. The section of line at summit level was the most exposed section in the Marches. *Ian Allan Library/ E. J. Dew*

Right:
Sentinel 0-4-0 No 47183 working at Clee Hill in spring 1950, carrying full British Railways lettering. *LGRP/Ian Allan Library*

MIDLAND

August Bank Holiday.

CHEAP EXCURSION TO SOUTH WALES.

ON SATURDAY, AUGUST 2nd,

COOK'S CHEAP EXCURSION TO

HEREFORD, HAY, TALYLLYN, BRECON,

NEATH & SWANSEA

(For the MUMBLES and GOWER)

(Via WORCESTER),

For Excursions to the WEST OF ENGLAND, see other Midland bills.

For 3, 4, 6, 7. 10. or 13 Days, will run as under:—

FROM					a.m.	FROM				p.m.
WALSALL	...	...	...	...	10†27	BIRMINGHAM (New Street)	...	...	1 12
Aldridge	...	...	...	...	10†35	Camp Hill	...	...	...	12†38
Sutton Coldfield	...	...	...	...	10†47	Moseley	...	...	...	12†31
					p.m.	King's Heath	...	...	...	12†28
Saltley	...	...	...	...	12†48	King's Norton	...	...	1*12
						* Via Barnt Green.				

† Join Excursion Train at New Street.

THIRD CLASS FARES THERE AND BACK.

To HEREFORD.	To HAY.	To TALYLLYN.	To BRECON.	To NEATH or SWANSEA.
6/6	9/6	10/-	10/-	12/6

RETURN ARRANGEMENTS.

On Monday, August 4th, Tuesday, August 5th, Thursday, August 7th, Friday, August 8th, Monday, August 11th, or Thursday, August 14th.

From		From		From	
SWANSEA ...... 8.30 a.m. or 11. 5 a.m.		BRECON .... 10.30 a.m. or 1.10 p.m.		HAY .... 11.25 a.m. or 2. 9 p.m.	
NEATH .... 8.25 a.m. or 11.20 a.m.		TALYLLYN ... 10.50 a.m. or 1.25 p.m.		HEREFORD ... 12.57 p.m. or 3.10 p.m.	

CONDITIONS OF ISSUE OF TICKETS.

CHILDREN under three years of age, free; three years and under twelve, half-fares.

NOTICE.—The tickets are not transferable, and will be available only on the dates, by the trains, and at the stations named; if used on any other date, by any other train, or at any other station than those named, the tickets will be forfeited, and the full ordinary fare charged.

The Company give notice that tickets for this excursion are issued at a reduced rate, and subject to the condition that the Company shall not be liable for any loss, damage, injury, or delay to passengers, arising from any cause whatsoever.

Sixty pounds of luggage allowed free at the owner's risk.

List of STATIONS, OFFICES, &c.,

OF THE

MIDLAND RAILWAY CO. and THOS. COOK & SON

WHERE TICKETS MAY BE OBTAINED.

MIDLAND RAILWAY CO.

WALSALL—The Station.

BIRMINGHAM—New St. Station; "Swan" Office, New St.; 46, Snow Hill; 1, George St., Parade; 44, Hall St.; and 3, Edgbaston St.

And at the OTHER STATIONS shewn herein.

Handbills can also be obtained at BIRMINGHAM at the Midland Parcels Receiving Offices in various parts of the town. TICKETS ISSUED ANY TIME IN ADVANCE.

THOS. COOK & SON.

WALSALL—21, Park Street.

BIRMINGHAM—Stephenson Place; 52 and 54, Corporation Street; and 161, Soho Road.

MIDLAND FOLDERS, giving particulars of the Company's Services, Luggage, Parcels, &c., arrangements, may be had on application at any Midland Station or Agency.

The Midland Company's Illustrated Annual, "Country and Seaside Holidays," with Directory of Furnished Apartments in Country and Seaside Districts for 1913, may be obtained at Midland Stations and Bookstalls, &c.

Information with regard to the Company's arrangements can be obtained from the District Passenger Agent, Midland Railway, New Street Station, Birmingham.

Derby, July, 1913.

W.B. 124-1913. (5497.)

W. GUY GRANET, General Manager.

Thos. Cook & Son, Printers, London and Birmingham.

For Steamship Passenger Information, apply at Cook's Shipping, &c., Offices, Walsall and Birmingham.

Left:
Lengthy journey times were a handicap to Midland Railway efforts to exploit the Hereford, Hay & Brecon route to South Wales. Passengers buying Cook's cheap excursion tickets during the August Bank Holiday in 1913 left Walsall at 10.27am but it was almost three hours later before they departed from Birmingham New Street. The tickets were valid for return journeys between three and 13 days later. *Author's collection*

Right:
A comprehensive 24-page excursion booklet issued by the Western Region divisional headquarters, Cardiff, with cover drawings suggesting steam was still dominant. *Author's collection*

Programme of REGULAR CHEAP EXCURSION BOOKINGS Weekdays & Sundays

From

HEREFORD
LEOMINSTER, LUDLOW
CRAVEN ARMS & STOKESAY

17th JUNE - 8th SEPTEMBER 1963

Above:
A wanderer far from its birth-place – ex-L&Y 0-6-0 No 52525 at Three Cocks on a Brecon-Hereford train soon after Nationalisation. London Midland Region timetables at that time showed four weekday-only trains each way, taking about 90 minutes for the 38-mile journey – timings almost identical with those of the Midland Railway in Edwardian days.
Ian Allan Library/R. W. Miller

Above left:
Bishop's Castle Railway second class issue of 1933 – two years before total closure.

Left:
Craven Arms & Stokesay to Hereford. 1943.

6. Locomotives and Sheds

Although GWR locomotives dominated the main lines and branches between the Mersey and the Wye, there was one touch of splendour they could not match – the sight of an LMS 'Coronation' streamliner at Shrewsbury on a running-in turn from Crewe Works. In fresh livery, they looked magnificent and it is fascinating to wonder whether the GWR might have been tempted to try to keep them out of sight when a chocolate and cream express was due. But such a thought is easily banished from the mind, for the streamliners often stood in a middle road at the station, in an historic setting far grander than any at Crewe.

At Shrewsbury, GWR 'Castle' class 4-6-0s were seen every day, looking majestic rather than speedy, arriving or departing with West of England, Birkenhead and Aberystwyth expresses, which they worked as far as here.

The 'Castles' had charge of the Paddington trains for almost a third of their journeys: from Chester to Wolverhampton Low Level – 72 miles of the 210-mile route. Between Birkenhead and Chester the expresses were in the charge of smaller locomotives, and from Wolverhampton to Paddington they were headed by 'King' class 4-6-0s.

Writing in *The Railway Magazine* about wartime locomotive working on the GWR, O. S. Nock said that the 215$\frac{1}{2}$ miles between Newton Abbot

Below:
The Shrewsbury & Crewe main line was frequently used for running-in turns. LMS 'Coronation' No 6224 *Princess Alexandra* takes water from an overhead gantry pipe at the north end of Shrewsbury station. *Ian Allan Library*

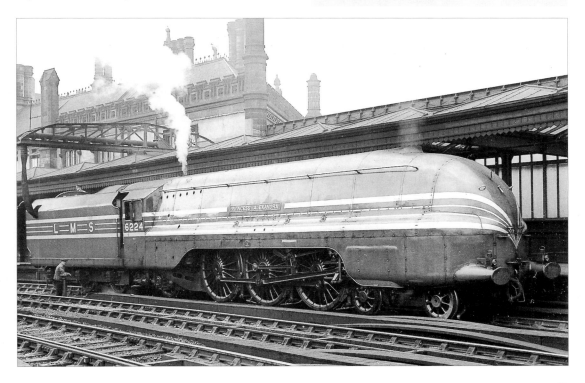

Above
Shrewsbury's GWR and LNWR sheds at Coleham
were built jointly as one but when relations
became strained a dividing wall was built, as
happened at Birkenhead on the joint line.
At Shrewsbury the LNWR shed was closest to the
Hereford main line. In about 1900 it housed
several different classes. An 0-8-0 is stabled
between a 2-4-2 tank and a 2-4-0 tender
locomotive – all Webb designs. The photograph
was taken from the large coal stack.
Ian Allan Library

and Shrewsbury were notable for the variety of
running conditions, loadings and gradients. 'As
in the last war, so in the present emergency the
West to North route via the Severn Tunnel has
provided an absorbing study for connoisseurs
of locomotive performance; many of the point-
to-point timings are but little eased from pre-
war days while generally train loads are vastly
heavier.' Recording footplate runs, he noted
that the expresses used Newton Abbot engines
on alternate days.

At Nationalisation, there were seven 'Castles'
and four 'Stars' among the allocation of 57
locomotives at Shrewsbury GWR shed. Chester
had five 'Saints' and one 'Castle' among 51;
Hereford had eight 'Saints' and one 'Castle' –
but a famous one: No 4079 *Pendennis Castle*.

Never allocated named locomotives were a
host of small sub-sheds dotted throughout the
Marches such as Kington, home of two 0-4-2
tanks, and Leominster which had four. At
Grouping three tank engines allocated to
Gobowen for working Oswestry motor trains
were transferred to Oswestry shed.

The biggest variety of locomotives was often
found at sheds which housed predominantly
heavy goods locomotives and shunters. At
Croes Newydd, Wrexham, in the fork of the
Shrewsbury and Chester main line and Brymbo
branches, its largest allocation was pannier
tanks, representing about one third of its 1947
roster.

It was one of the interesting conjectures of
local railway history, that had not war broken
out in 1939, the GWR might have built another

Above:
Two GWR 'County' class 4-6-0s and a 'Castle': Nos 1017 *County of Hereford*, 4037 *The South Wales Borderers* and 1013 *County of Dorset* at Shrewsbury shed on 13 September 1958.
Ian Allan Library

Right:
Drifting past the Shrewsbury sheds with a heavy mineral train from South Wales is Churchward 2-8-0 No 2845 on 14 September 1959.
Ian Allan Library

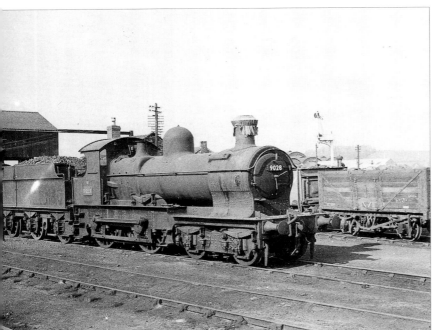

Left:
Craven Arms was among a number of widely scattered sub-sheds of Shrewsbury. In spring 1957, ex-GWR 4-4-0 No 9028 was stored outside. It was in filthy condition with a capped chimney and full tender. *R. C. Blaker*

Below:
GWR Croes Newydd shed, a short distance south of Wrexham General station, was noted for the variety of its locomotives. The roundhouse in summer 1964 with 0-6-0 pannier tank No 9610, BR Standard 4-6-0 No 75071, BR Standard 2-6-2 tank No 84000, the first of a class which was a tank version of the 78000 series of 2-6-0s, and GWR 0-6-2 tank No 5677. *Ian Allan Library*

large shed. An internal company report of 1924 mentioned plans for a shed at Saltney, saying that it was not possible before 1938 because of a brick company's rights to work clay under the site until then. It is not clear whether the shed would have replaced the existing one or whether it was intended to service heavy freight locomotives which worked in and out of Saltney marshalling yard, a hidden gem of Paddington's presence at Chester. At Birkenhead, small tanks, mainly for shunting the docks, totalled about half of the depot's locomotive allocation.

The locomotives at the LMS sheds at

Shrewsbury, Chester and Birkenhead were similar in type to those of the GWR. 'Jubilee' class 4-6-0s were the biggest locomotives stationed at Shrewsbury in the latter days of steam, but 'Royal Scots' and other 4-6-0s shared express duties over the Shrewsbury & Hereford line.

Chester LMS shed was not large because most freight locomotives were allocated to Mold Junction and its position was somewhat isolated, but the GWR was able to stamp its personality on the city, not only by being joint owner of General station but also having its large locomotive shed at the platform end.

Spotters usually visited sheds because of the variety of locomotives to be found there, rather than for shed buildings, which were almost universally ugly. There was little scenic charm in Wrexham's railways, but they did have admirers for years and one group of enthusiasts visited Rhosddu, the former Great Central shed, on New Year's Day, because they said it was the only day of the year on which they could be

Below:
Croes Newydd shed c1967 shortly before closure. Nearest the camera is 'Black Five' No 44872. The shed is on the left and the single track in the foreground was a spur between the main line and the Brymbo branch. Wrexham South Fork signalbox is behind the signals. *Ian Allan Library/A. O. Wynn*

sure of finding the locomotives they wanted to see. The rest of the time the small tanks were scattered over miles of branches.

Oswestry, the largest of the Cambrian sheds, became the headquarters of a GWR locomotive division stretching from Whitchurch to the Cambrian coast and Brecon. A time-warped picture of the Oswestry scene was provided in a report by a member of the Railway Correspondence and Travel Society, who wrote of a visit to the shed on a May evening in 1938.

In the shed and yard he found eight 0-6-0s: four ex-Cambrian and four Deans. He noted that No 893, although lately out of shops, had developed cylinder trouble and was due to return to Swindon the next day. Also on shed were three 4-4-0s and the Cambrian 2-4-0Ts Nos 1196 and 1197. No 1308 *Lady Margaret* had returned to Oswestry after overhaul and was working on the Tanat Valley line.

Locomotive Works

The shed was just across the OE&W line from the former Cambrian works – the only ones of any size in the Border country. Only two locomotives were ever built there but many were extensively rebuilt.

The works, for which over 4 million bricks were needed, were dominated by a 150ft high chimney and the tower of the main building was topped by a fine weather vane of an 'Albion' class 2-4-0, one of the earliest passenger classes to be built by Sharp, Stewart & Co, about the same time as the works were completed.

From the town centre the works were reached by a footbridge, just north of the station, which spanned nine Cambrian and four GWR tracks. The works handled locomotive, carriages and wagons, the locomotive section being the largest.

Right:
Oswestry was by far the biggest of the Cambrian sheds, with more than 30 locomotives allocated. Shortly before Nationalisation they were made up of nine classes including 13 0-6-0s and two 'Manor' class 4-6-0s. Cambrian 4-4-0s Nos 70 and 72 stand outside with well-filled tenders, c1900. *R. W. Miller*

Centre right:
Oswestry shed on 15 May 1938 with three locomotives identified as GWR Nos 2481, 2075 and 680. The single main line to Whitchurch, straight as an arrow, heads into the distance. *R. W. Miller*

Below right:
Hereford LNWR/LMS shed in July 1935 where W. A. Camwell found 'Prince of Wales' class 4-6-0s Nos 25726 and 25672 and Aspinall ex-L&Y 0-6-0s Nos 12131 and 12118. *Stephenson Locomotive Society/W. A. Camwell*

Left:
Rhosddu – the Wrexham, Mold & Connah's Quay shed in the Great Central era with, left, Cambrian 0-6-0 No 79. In the centre are three WM&CQR saddle tanks with No 40 behind, standing just outside the shed. Relations between the WM&CQ and Cambrian were strengthened when some locomotives were sent to Oswestry for heavy repairs. *Ian Allan Library*

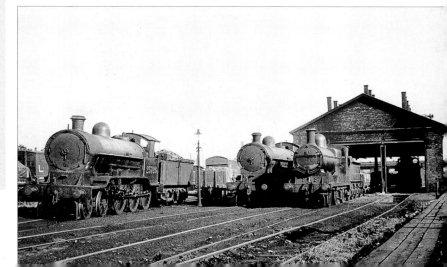

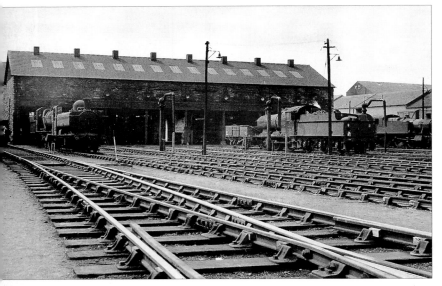

Left:
Hereford GWR shed (1853-1964) had an allocation of more than 40 locomotives at nationalisation. They included 'Saint' and 'Hall' 4-6-0s but the largest single type comprised 0-6-0 pannier tanks. *Stephenson Locomotive Society/W. A. Camwell*

Centre left:
Oswestry Works c1921 with 0-4-4 tank No 9, 4-4-0 No 11 and 4-4-0 No 94 or 96. An example of the cramped conditions in which locomotives were repaired. A central transverser switched 12 roads. *R. W. Miller*

Below left:
The carriage works where a wide variety of coaches were built and repaired, including those which the Cambrian bought from outside contractors. *R. W. Miller*

Above:
About 1925, GWR 'Duke' class
4-4-0 No 3256 *Guinevere* pilots
a Cambrian Jones 4-4-0 on a
heavy goods train passing the
works. *R. W. Miller*

Right:
Oswestry Works on 26 May
1953 with the 4.5pm
Whitchurch-Welshpool
headed by BR Class 2 2-6-0
No 78005 – six months after
the class was introduced.
R. W. Miller

Left:
The loneliest of the border sheds was Clee Hill, a wooden structure well buttressed against gales sweeping the summit level of the Ludlow & Clee Hill branch. Locomotives used on the branch and incline were also serviced at the single-road Ludlow LNWR shed, which was a sub-shed of Shrewsbury. *Ian Allan Library*

Below:
The Cambrian stabled one or two locomotives at Whitchurch, an LNWR sub-shed of Crewe, seen here in 1955. The LMS and BR used Whitchurch to service locomotives on running-in turns from Crewe Works. *Ian Allan Library*

Chronology

Openings and closures: main lines and main branches. (Important dates only.)

Chester

Chester-Birkenhead Grange Lane	Birkenhead, Lancashire & Cheshire Junction (BL&CJR)	23 September 1840
Extension to Birkenhead Woodside		1 April 1878
Chester-Crewe	Grand Junction Railway	1 October 1840
Chester-Saltney Jct	Chester & Holyhead	4 November 1846
Chester (Saltney Jct)-Ruabon	Shrewsbury & Chester	4 November 1846
Chester General station Joint Committee		1 August 1848
Saltney Jct-Mold	Chester & Holyhead	14 August 1849
Chester-Warrington (Walton Jct)	BL&CJR	18 December 1850
Waverton (Tattenhall Jct)-Whitchurch	LNWR	1 October 1872

Cheshire Lines Committee

Chester (Northgate)-Mouldsworth		2 November 1874 Goods
		1 May 1875 Passengers

Great Central Railway

Chester Northgate-Hawarden Bridge		31 March 1890

Passenger Service Withdrawals

Chester General-Whitchurch		16 September 1957
Chester General-Mold/Denbigh		30 April 1962
Chester Northgate-Hawarden Bridge		9 September 1968
Chester Northgate-Mickle Trafford Jct and Northgate station		6 October 1969

Wrexham and Ruabon

Chester (Saltney Jct)-Wrexham-Ruabon	S&CR	4 November 1846
Wrexham-Minera	S&CR	July 1847
Ruabon-Llangollen	Vale of Llangollen	1 December 1861
Wrexham-Buckley	Wrexham, Mold & Connah's Quay	1 May 1866
Brymbo-Llanfynydd	LNWR/GWR Joint	27 January 1872
Wrexham: Moss Valley branch	GWR	11 May 1882
Wrexham-Brymbo	WM&CQR	1882-7
Wrexham Exchange-Wrexham Central	WM&CQR	1 November 1887
Wrexham Central-Ellesmere	Cambrian Railways (worked)	2 November 1895

Through Routes Completed

Shrewsbury & Chester		14 October 1848

Wrexham Central-Hawarden Bridge-Chester Northgate		31 March 1890
Wrexham Central-Hawarden Bridge-Seacombe & Egremont		31 March 1896
Ruabon-Barmouth Junction		21 June 1869

Passenger Service Withdrawals

Ruabon-Legacy (Ponkey branch)		22 March 1915
Wrexham Central-Brymbo (WM&CQR)		1 March 1917
Wrexham General-Brymbo-Berwig Halt		1 January 1931
Wrexham General-Rhos		1 January 1931 Excursions ran to 1950
Wrexham General-Moss Valley		1 January 1931
Brymbo-Llanfynydd		27 March 1950
Wrexham Central-Ellesmere		10 September 1962
Ruabon-Llangollen		18 January 1965

Oswestry

Oswestry-Gobowen	S&CR	23 December 1848
Oswestry-Welshpool	O&NR	14 August 1860
Llanymynech-Llanfyllin	O&NR	17 July 1863
Oswestry-Whitchurch	OE&WR	27 July 1864
Porthywaen-Llangynog	Cambrian	5 January 1904

Through Routes Completed

Whitchurch-Aberystwyth	Cambrian	27 July 1864
Dovey Junction-Pwllheli	Cambrian	10 October 1867

Passenger Service Withdrawals

Oswestry-Llangynog		15 January 1951
Oswestry-Welshpool		18 January 1965
Oswestry-Whitchurch		18 January 1965
Oswestry-Llanfyllin		18 January 1965
Oswestry-Gobowen		7 November 1966

Shrewsbury

Shrewsbury & Chester	GWR	14 October 1848
Shrewsbury-Wellington	LNWR-GWR Joint	1 June 1849
Shrewsbury-Hereford	LNWR-GWR Joint	6 December 1853
Shrewsbury-Crewe	LNWR	1 September 1858
Hanwood-Minsterley	LNWR/GWR Joint	14 February 1861
Shrewsbury-Welshpool	LNWR/GWR Joint	27 January 1862
Shrewsbury (Abbey)-Llanymynech	S&MR	13 August 1866
Shrewsbury: Abbey curve	LNWR/GWR Joint	1 May 1867

Through Routes Completed

Shrewsbury-Birmingham New Street	1 February 1854
Shrewsbury-Newport NA&HR	16 January 1854
Worcester-Hereford	13 September 1861

Passenger Service Withdrawals

Shrewsbury (Abbey)-Llanymynech	6 November 1933 Specials ran until 31 December 1959
Minsterley branch	5 February 1951

Hereford

Hereford, Abergavenny & Newport Railway	16 January 1854
Hereford, Ross & Gloucester Railway	2 June 1855
Hereford & Worcester Railway	13 September 1861
Hereford, Hay and Brecon Railway	18 September 1864

Shrewsbury & Hereford Branches

Leominster-Kington	GWR	27 July 1857
Craven Arms-Swansea	LNWR	1861-1867
Woofferton-Tenbury (Station renamed Tenbury Wells 14 November 1912)	LNWR/GWR Joint	1 August 1861
Shrewsbury-Hartlebury	GWR	1 February 1862
Tenbury-Bewdley	GWR	13 August 1864
Ludlow-Clee Hill	L&CHR	24 August 1864
Hereford-Brecon	HH&BR	19 September 1864
Craven Arms-Bishop's Castle	BCR	24 October 1865
Craven Arms (Marsh Farm Jct)-Buildwas	GWR	18 December 1867
Titley-Eardisley	GWR	3 August 1874
Titley-Presteign	GWR	10 September 1875
Kington-New Radnor	GWR	25 September 1875
Leominster-Worcester	GWR	1 September 1897

Passenger Service Withdrawals

Craven Arms-Bishop's castle (complete closure) 20 April 1935

Titley-Eardisley	1 July 1940
Leominster-Presteign	5 February 1951
Craven Arms-Much Wenlock	31 December 1951
Leominster-New Radnor	7 February 1955
Woofferton-Tenbury	31 July 1961
Tenbury-Bewdley	1 August 1962
Hereford-Brecon	31 December 1962
Leominster-Worcester	7 September 1964
Shrewsbury-Hartlebury	9 January 1970
Clee Hill Incline	7 November 1960
Ludlow-Bitterley	31 December 1962

Bibliography

As well as *Bradshaw's Manuals* and timetables, working timetables and books mentioned in the text, I also consulted:

G. F. Bannister, *Branch Line Byways: Central Wales*, Atlantic Transport Publishers, 1987.

D. S. M. Barrie, *Regional History of Railways: Vol 12 South Wales*, David & Charles, 1980.

Peter E. Baughan, *Regional History of Railways: Vol 11 North and Mid Wales*, David & Charles, 1980.

K. M. Beck, *The Great Western North of Wolverhampton*, Ian Allan, 1986.

A. Bodlander, M. Hambly, H. Leadbetter, D. Southern and S. Weatherley, *Wrexham Railways: A Collection of Pictures*, Bridge Books, 1992 and 1993.

A. Bodlander, M. Hambly, H. Leadbetter and D. Southern, *Oswestry Railways: A Collection of Pictures*, Bridge Books, 1994.

Rex Christiansen, *Forgotten Railways: North and Mid Wales*, David & Charles, 1976.

Rex Christiansen, *Forgotten Railways: Severn Valley and the Welsh Border*, David & Charles, 1988.

Rex Christiansen and R. W. Miller, *The Cambrian Railways*, two volumes, David & Charles, 1967 and 1969.

Clinker's Register of Closed Passenger Stations and Goods Depots 1830-1977, Avon Anglia, 1978.

R. A. Cooke, *Atlas of the Great Western Railway 1947*, Wild Swan, 1988. This provided an invaluable coverage of the Welsh border lines and I strongly recommend it as a stimulating source for recapturing memories.

Nigel Dyckhoff, *Portrait of the Cheshire Lines Committee*, Ian Allan, 1999.

Chris Hawkins and George Reeve, *LMS Engine Sheds: Vol 1 The L&NWR*, Wild Swan Publications, 1981.

G. C. Lewthwaite: *Branch Line Index* (3rd edition), Branch Line Society, 1991.

E. Lyons, *An Historical Survey of Great Western Engine Sheds 1947*, Oxford Publishing Company, 1972.